Reappraising Local and Community News in the UK

T0347965

Drawing on expert contributions from around the UK, this collection brings together a series of insights into the contemporary local and community news media landscape in the UK.

Offering an analysis of the ongoing "crisis" in the provision of local news, exacerbated by the COVID-19 pandemic, the book provides a critical space for practitioners and scholars to reflect on emerging models for economically sustainable, participatory local news services. It showcases new scholarly analyses of local news provision and community news practices, giving voice to the experiences of practitioners from across the local news ecology. In a set of diverse contributing chapters, campaigners and practitioners map out the period of recent rapid change for local news, questioning contemporary government initiatives and highlighting the advent of diverse, entrepreneurial reactions to the spaces created by a decline in local mainstream news services. This book is a timely examination of what we can learn from the variety of approaches being taken across the local media landscape in the commercial, subsidised, and non-profit sector, shining new light on how practices that place the engagement of citizens at their centre might be propagated within this policy and funding landscape.

Reappraising Local and Community News in the UK is a valuable resource for students and scholars interested in local news and journalism, as well as for anyone interested in the evolving local media landscape in the UK.

David Harte is an associate professor within the Birmingham Institute of Media and English at Birmingham City University. He is co-author of *Hyperlocal Journalism*, published by Routledge. He has published widely on community and hyperlocal media, as well as running his own hyperlocal news website in Birmingham since 2010.

Rachel Matthews is Associate Head of the School of Media and Performing Arts at Coventry University. A former journalist, her research focuses on the local newspaper – past, present, and future. She is the author of *A History of the Provincial Press* in England published by Bloomsbury Academic.

Disruptions: Studies in Digital Journalism
Series editor: Bob Franklin

Disruptions refers to the radical changes provoked by the affordances of digital technologies that occur at a pace and on a scale that disrupts settled understandings and traditional ways of creating value, interacting and communicating both socially and professionally. The consequences for digital journalism involve far reaching changes to business models, professional practices, roles, ethics, products and even challenges to the accepted definitions and understandings of journalism. For Digital Journalism Studies, the field of academic inquiry which explores and examines digital journalism, disruption results in paradigmatic and tectonic shifts in scholarly concerns. It prompts reconsideration of research methods, theoretical analyses and responses (oppositional and consensual) to such changes, which have been described as being akin to 'a moment of mind-blowing uncertainty'.

Routledge's new book series, *Disruptions: Studies in Digital Journalism*, seeks to capture, examine and analyse these moments of exciting and explosive professional and scholarly innovation which characterize developments in the day-to-day practice of journalism in an age of digital media, and which are articulated in the newly emerging academic discipline of Digital Journalism Studies.

Disrupting Sports Journalism
Simon McEnnis

Disruption and Digital Journalism
Assessing News Media Innovation in a Time of Dramatic Change
John V. Pavlik

For more information, please visit: www.routledge.com/Disruptions/book-series/DISRUPTDIGJOUR

Reappraising Local and Community News in the UK

Media, Practice, and Policy

**Edited by David Harte
and Rachel Matthews**

Routledge
Taylor & Francis Group

LONDON AND NEW YORK

First published 2022
by Routledge
2 Park Square, Milton Park, Abingdon, Oxon OX14 4RN

and by Routledge
605 Third Avenue, New York, NY 10158

Routledge is an imprint of the Taylor & Francis Group, an informa business

© 2022 selection and editorial matter, David Harte and Rachel Matthews
individual chapters, the contributors

The right of David Harte and Rachel Matthews to be identified as the authors
of the editorial material, and of the authors for their individual chapters,
has been asserted in accordance with sections 77 and 78 of the Copyright,
Designs and Patents Act 1988.

All rights reserved. No part of this book may be reprinted or reproduced or utilised
in any form or by any electronic, mechanical, or other means, now known or
hereafter invented, including photocopying and recording, or in any information
storage or retrieval system, without permission in writing from the publishers.

Trademark notice: Product or corporate names may be trademarks or registered
trademarks, and are used only for identification and explanation without
intent to infringe.

British Library Cataloguing-in-Publication Data
A catalogue record for this book is available from the British Library

Library of Congress Cataloging-in-Publication Data
Names: Harte, David, 1968– editor. | Matthews, Rachel, 1967– editor.
Title: Reappraising local and community news in the UK : media,
practice and policy / edited by David Harte and Rachel Matthews.
Description: London ; New York : Routledge, 2022. |
Series: Disruptions: studies in digital journalism |
Includes bibliographical references and index.
Identifiers: LCCN 2021023751 | ISBN 9781032001883 (hardback) |
ISBN 9781003173144 (ebook)
Subjects: LCSH: Journalism, Regional–Great Britain. |
Online journalism–Great Britain.
Classification: LCC PN5124.R44 R43 2022 | DDC 072–dc23
LC record available at https://lccn.loc.gov/2021023751

ISBN: 9781032001883 (hbk)
ISBN: 9781032001890 (pbk)
ISBN: 9781003173144 (ebk)

DOI: 10.4324/9781003173144

Typeset in Times New Roman
by Newgen Publishing UK

Contents

Figures

Tables

Contributors

Julia Boelle, Cardiff University
Julia Boelle is a recent PhD graduate of Cardiff University's School of Journalism, Media and Culture. Her research interests are situated in the fields of disaster and crisis communications. In the past year, she has worked on two community journalism projects, focusing on the experiences of community journalists and successful funding models.

Sarah Cheverton, University of Portsmouth
Sarah is currently undertaking a PhD at the University of Portsmouth's Faculty of Creative and Cultural Industries, researching the "crisis" facing local and community journalism. Since 2015, she has run a community news website in Portsmouth, *Star & Crescent.*

Josephine F. Coleman, Brunel University
Josephine is a lecturer in Media and Public Relations at Brunel University, London. As a practitioner-academic, her interdisciplinary research interests include local media and communities, digital content production, and journalistic practice. She is Communications Officer for MeCCSA Radio Studies Network.

Clare Cook, University of Central Lancashire
Clare is a senior lecturer at the School of Journalism and Arts at the University of Central Lancashire. Her focus is on the business aspects of independent and community publishing through action and applied research. She publishes primarily in the media management field.

Mark Dunford, DigiTales
Mark is a director of DigiTales, a media production company hosted by the Institute of Cultural and Creative Entrepreneurship at Goldsmiths College University of London. His research explores

participatory media practices and he was a contributing editor of *Digital Storytelling Form and Content* (Palgrave Macmillan, 2017).

Iñaki Garcia-Blanco, Cardiff University

Iñaki is a senior lecturer at the School of Journalism, Media and Culture (Cardiff University). Currently, he is undertaking research on hyperlocal/community journalism in the UK. His work appears in journals such as *Journalism, Journalism Studies, Media, Culture & Society* and *Feminist Media Studies*.

Agnes Gulyas, Canterbury Christ Church University

Agnes is Professor of Media and Communications and Director of Research and Enterprise in the School of Creative Arts and Industries at Canterbury Christ Church University. She has published widely on local media and digital journalism, including her recent co-edited volume *The Routledge Companion to Local Media and Journalism*.

Jonathan Heawood, Public Interest News Foundation

Jonathan is Executive Director of the Public Interest News Foundation and a Senior Research Fellow in the Philosophy Department at the University of Stirling. He established the UK's first independent press regulator, IMPRESS, and has published a monograph on media regulation, *The Press Freedom Myth* (Biteback 2019).

Aleksandar Kocic, Edinburgh Napier University

Aleksandar is a journalism lecturer at Edinburgh Napier University and a radio journalist. His research interests include local news, local radio, public service media, and news literacy. He is vice-chair of MeCCSA Radio Studies Network.

Coral Milburn-Curtis, University of Oxford

Coral is an Associate Fellow of Green Templeton, University of Oxford, where she teaches Quantitative Research Methods, specialising in survey design and analysis and structural equation modelling. She is a professor and Director of Studies for the Doctor of Business Administration (DBA) programme at Pôle Paris Alternance, a Paris Business School.

Jelena Milicev, University of Glasgow

Jelena is undertaking a PhD in social and public health sciences at the University of Glasgow. She is using mixed methods and social network analysis to look at student social support and well-being. She worked as a reporter in local media for a number of years.

Jerry Padfield, Falmouth University

Jerry is a PhD student at Falmouth University in the Environmental Futures programme, where he is researching ways to broaden participation in community radio and podcasting practice as a means to improve mental well-being. He is an Early Career Research Development Officer for the MeCCSA Radio Studies Network.

Jingrong Tong, University of Sheffield

Dr Jingrong Tong is Senior Lecturer in Digital News Cultures at the University of Sheffield. Her current research focuses on digital technology and journalism, social data analysis, and environmental communication.

Karin Wahl-Jorgensen, Cardiff University

Karin Wahl-Jorgensen is Director of Research for the Centre for Community Journalism at Cardiff University, where she is also University Dean of Research Environment and Culture and a professor in the School of Journalism, Media and Culture. She has published extensively in the field of journalism studies.

Introduction

Local public service journalism and the BBC

David Harte

Introduction

In early 2021, the *Plymouth Live* news website (the online presence of *Plymouth News*, owned by Reach PLC, one of the UK's largest newspaper groups) published a news story about a small number of domestic rubbish bins that had fallen over during some windy weather. "Scenes of devastation in Stoke after wind wreaks havoc with wheelie bins" ran the headline (Dorwick 2021b). Published as both a short news story and in a live blogging format, readers were invited to send in their own updates and photographs of dustbins (which many did). The story seemed exactly the kind of example that the online blog, Facebook group, and later book, *Angry People in local newspapers* (Coleman 2018) would consider worthy of lampooning. It would be a little extreme to call it "one of the dullest stories ever committed to print" (Coleman 2018: 2) but it is certainly, at first glance at least, rather banal. It is local, but is it news? Yet on closer inspection, it's clear that the story is sending itself up – "one kind Samaritan has bravely faced the wind to pick up her wheelie bin" (Dorwick 2021b) – with the journalist later admitting the story was something of a joke (Dorwick 2021c) and in terms of engagement with audiences, was "doing alright" (Dorwick 2021a).

This example hints at the journey that local news has taken in the digital era. While a story of wheelie bins being blown over may have made, at best, a "news in brief" in a printed newspaper, online it is required to "do alright" by driving traffic to *Plymouth Live's* website. If satirising local news can result in more clicks than writing the story straight – as part of a "culture of the click" (Anderson 2011: 555) strategy – then so be it. As David Higgerson, the digital editorial strategy director of Reach PLC, points out, page views are everything: "the page view, which triggers the revenue, which funds the journalism" (2019). What local news has to do is create content that is "written to perform

DOI: 10.4324/9781003173144-1

well in search and social" but which might be primarily there to "amuse and entertain readers" (Higgerson 2015). Such content, as beyond parody as some of it may seem, whether scholars and commentators like it or not, plays a vital role in sustaining the business of local news: "[they] provide the financial support through advertising to support the journalism which people expect from us, but which we have to work harder to get people to engage with" (Higgerson 2017). Although many digital news strategies are aimed at getting audiences to click on any kind of content in order to get eyeballs on online advertising, that is not the whole picture. This book looks at the local and community media sector's attempts to continue to produce the journalism people "expect" at a time when established business models continue to be disrupted by digital transformation and a global pandemic has brought into sharp focus the need for trusted, local news that keeps citizens informed and holds local power to account. This introduction sets out a rationale for reappraising local and community news at this point in time, with particular attention to the role of state subsidy for local public service journalism via the BBC.

Reappraising local and community news

The need for a reappraisal of local and community news is timely. Kristy Hess has contended that local newspapers hold "a degree of symbolic power in constructing the idea of 'community' and the 'local'" (Hess and Waller 2012: 56), but more recent research has suggested that the monopoly that legacy news brands had on defining the concept of local news has become ambiguous. The result is that there is: "no shared understanding among audience members about what local news is in the digital environment" (Gulyas et al. 2019: 1859). Further, despite attempts by publishers to create effective digital titles built on the reputation of longstanding local newspaper brands, Dame Frances Cairncross made the case that the transition to online has resulted in commercial local news publications becoming "less essential to community life" (Department for Digital, Culture, Media and Sport 2019: 80). The availability of alternative spaces for local news and information – not least on social media with new entrants (such as *Nextdoor*) starting to make inroads in a market dominated by Facebook – poses a further threat to the status of the local press as the most significant element in local public spheres of information: "Facebook groups, political parties, local enterprises, schools, and churches now represent important supplements, and sometimes serious competition, to traditional local news online as they provide important hyperlocal information" (Newman et al. 2020: 48).

While Cairncross (Department for Digital, Culture, Media and Sport 2019) outlined in stark terms the potential damage to democratic participation by citizens if local news media continue to retract in scale and scope, the picture from news publishers themselves can often feel a little contradictory. Regional newspaper owners may well be closing offices (Tobitt 2021b) but they are also lauding the growth in number of their local titles, in digital form at least (Sharman 2021c). Online audiences are growing, particularly during the COVID-19 pandemic (Tobitt 2021a), yet print still matters in business terms. Despite a significant decline in revenue from their print titles in 2020, the largest UK regional news publisher Reach PLC still relies heavily on newspaper sales and print advertising income where it accounts for 71% of their total revenue (Tobitt 2021c). In general, the UK news industry continues to make profits from their businesses (Edge 2019) and have shown "remarkable resiliency" (35), largely through a programme of rationalisation that continued in 2020 with 550 jobs cut by Reach and a "more centralised structure for editorial" (Ponsford and Mayhew 2021) put in place. The organisation of newsrooms that supply local content to print and digital titles is changing, with roles such as "engagement producer" and "SEO [search engine optimisation] content editor" now sitting alongside reporter roles in editorial jobs listings (Sharman 2021b). The focus in the regional commercial press emphasises a model of "the page view, which triggers the revenue" (Higgerson 2019) but experiments with other income-generation models are increasing (Mayhew 2021).

This experimentation is evident internationally too ("news organisations across Europe and in the US are challenging the assumption that people will not pay," Simon and Graves 2019: 5) and although we focus on the UK for our reappraisal, it's clear the issue of sustaining local journalism is of concern in many western democracies (Moore 2014: 27). Just as in the UK, where Agnes Gulyas (Chapter 1) points out that it is the areas of highest economic deprivation where the gaps in provision of local and regional newspapers are emerging, access to trusted local news is also a major area of concern in the US. The appearance of news deserts there is seen as the result of two decades worth of "successive technological and economic assaults [that] have destroyed the for-profit business model that sustained local journalism in this country for two centuries" (Abernathy 2020: 8). As if the picture painted wasn't gloomy enough, the author adds: "Then, the coronavirus hit" (ibid.). Damian Radcliffe makes the point that "COVID-19 has accelerated long-term financial trends that have beset journalism, and in particular newspapers, for some time" (2020: par 6). Local US newspapers, or at least what's left of them, have also been dealing with "digital disruption" (Ali et al. 2019: 887). Yet here there are signs that owners, editors, and journalists are responding unevenly but increasingly effectively to the challenge of sustaining local news in the digital age. Likewise, in Europe, recent research (Jenkins and Jeronimo 2021; Jenkins and Nielsen 2020) examining editorial and structural changes in local regional newspapers has noted how editors and journalists retain a public service ethos during the process of adapting to the impact of digital disruption. Journalists have been required to act more flexibly and shift to "aligning their journalistic ideals with consumers' interests" (Jenkins and Jeronimo 2021: 15). Owners meanwhile have been required to adjust "company expectations about success" (ibid.). In some ways, managers and editors have to look backwards and forwards during a period of dynamic transformation whereby print publications still generate the majority of revenues while the digital presents them with both challenges and opportunities for innovation (Jenkins and Nielsen 2020). Across Europe: "the challenge they face is to balance preservation of a legacy editorial and commercial product in inexorable structural decline with the evolution of new, digitally native editorial and commercial products" (2020: 485).

Private and public funding for local public interest news

If our reappraisal comes at a time when business models for local news are shifting, it is also clear that public interest journalism in UK newspapers has found itself having to be supported through subsidy and philanthropy. This has arrived through both the diversion of existing public funds (via the BBC's Local News Partnerships scheme, discussed below) and through grant funding from the companies that were central to the erosion of newspaper advertising revenue in the first place. Google has had a range of funding schemes open to applications from mainstream publishers via their Digital News Initiative, set up in 2015. Mainstream regional newspapers have a good track record of securing funds from Google for project work and in 2020, some local titles secured monies from a Google-funded emergency COVID-19 fund that was aimed largely at ensuring that basic reporting could continue (Sharman 2021d). In 2019, Facebook partnered with the National Union of Journalists to fund 83 regional journalists in a project intended to improve newsroom diversity and coverage of under-reported communities (Sharman 2021a). Community news publishers have also been recipients of global funding for local journalism and in her chapter in this collection, Sarah Cheverton puts such monies to use to test participatory journalism approaches but is clear that it does little to ease underlying issues of precarity for community media organisations (see Chapter 4). The House of Lords Communications and Digital Committee report, *Breaking News? The Future of UK Journalism,* critiqued the disjointed nature of public and external funding for journalism, seeing a role for government which it felt should: "look to help to bring greater coherence to the various initiatives which financially support journalism. There are many promising schemes, both publicly and privately run, but there is scope for a more joined-up approach" (2020: 3).

Perhaps, the most significant initiative in the last few years has been the advent of the Local News Partnerships between the BBC and the UK regional news industry. Operating since 2017, this has involved three schemes where the BBC collaborates with and supports community and mainstream commercial regional news services. These are a news hub service allowing external media organisations access to BBC video news material for use online, a collaborative data journalism unit staffed by the BBC and seconded reporters from local news providers (discussed by Jingrong Tong in Chapter 7 of this book), and the Local Democracy Reporters (LDRS) scheme, involving 165 reporters (as of April 2021), covering the regular business and workings of local democratic institutions. The LDRS is perhaps the most significant of the Local News Partnerships, offering direct funding from the BBC for journalists to be situated in community and commercial newsrooms (in most cases, the latter). The scheme is due to run for the course of the current Royal Charter Period until 2027 and its origins can be traced back to the periods leading up to the renewal of the BBC's charter in 2006 and in 2016. As I outline below, these periods were marked by important debates about who is best placed to serve local news audiences and the degree to which local public service journalism should be subsidised.

Localism and the BBC

In 2004, the BBC set out its vision for the forthcoming Charter Period to begin in 2007 in a report called *Building public value: renewing the BBC for a digital world* (BBC 2004). As Paul Smith has noted (2009), although the period leading up to renewal had seen a repeat of well-rehearsed debates about competition and consumer choice, in general, the BBC benefitted from the then Labour Government's "underlying ideological support for the principles of public service broadcasting" (148). The proposal from the BBC that it should use digital technologies to "connect communities" was largely accepted (BBC 2004: 109). "Social and community value" (2004: 109) was one of five pillars of public value it saw itself contributing to, drawing on survey data to argue that "people increasingly value localness" (2004: 109). Its move to increase its local output and thus increase its impact in localities was based on two key reasons:

> First, ongoing pressure for devolution and local accountability will amplify the importance of effective representation of UK society in broadcasting. Second, commercial pressures are leading ITV to rationalise its regional infrastructure, a process that has already started following the merger of Granada and Carlton.
>
> (BBC 2004: 109)

Although the BBC's position was driven by its own consultation process with audiences, Ofcom's review of public service broadcasting at the time also noted that audiences "feel that 'regional' news is not 'local' enough" (Ofcom 2004: 57). The BBC's solution was an ambitious UK-wide "ultra-local" TV service (BBC 2004: 66). The BBC's rationale involved a critique of its existing regional news that is recognised as having to cover areas so large that for many viewers it failed to offer "truly relevant local news" (BBC 2004: 66). The plan was for 50–60 areas to be served with up to 10 minutes an hour of "genuinely relevant local news and information" (ibid.). The then Director-General of the BBC, Mark Thompson, outlined a vision of a service: "as local as our radio services, serving individual cities, conurbations and counties" (BBC 2005). Whilst local newspapers get no mention in the *Building public value report*, localism certainly does, with the promise of "a unique service that will reflect the lives and concerns of local communities" (ibid.).

The BBC went ahead with a pilot of its "ultra" local news in the West Midlands region (running for nine months from December 2005) which had, as with other regions, only a single regional TV news programme. A previous pilot scheme for local television in Hull (between 2001 and 2005) informed the West Midlands service although it had operated on slightly different terms, involving direct collaboration and interaction with the community and community organisations, as well as a dedicated local news bulletin for the city and wider local area. The Hull pilot had drawn criticism from the main local newspaper that saw its status as the first choice for local news decline during the period of the pilot (Laughton 2006: 39). This criticism from the regional press would continue during the West Midlands pilot. Indeed, the Newspaper Society's criticism began even before the pilot had started: "the regional newspaper industry's ability to sustain its crucial role in its communities is at risk from the BBC's planned expansion in the local and regional media" (Newspaper Society 2005: par 5). Editors lined up to condemn the venture, arguing that this amounted to the BBC undertaking "parish-pump reporting" and accusing it of "an unwarranted appropriation of public money to expand into areas that are already well-served by existing media" (Press Gazette 2005). Once started, viewers themselves felt a little short-changed, critiquing the service as "local radio with pictures" (Hereford Times 2006).

Although it had some innovative aspects – including a partnership with the Community Media Association that saw amateur community filmmakers contribute short video inserts – the pilot was not rolled out further. An independent review argued that by and large the pilot had worked in enabling effective two-way partnerships between the BBC and community and civic organisations, and in contributing to ensuring a "plurality of voice into some local markets" (Laughton 2006: 40). Where it hadn't worked was in delivering value for money. It had also created "an uneasy relationship with the local press" (ibid.). The BBC management's own assessment (BBC 2008) of the value of the West Midlands' trial was that it had worked best in its participatory elements but that future local video proposals would be more attentive to partnering with other news providers. Thus, it set out a remit for its future "Local Video Proposals" (BBC 2008: 62) that created a template for what would become the Local News Partnerships. This would see the BBC: "making content available to other providers, […] purchasing local video news, […] link generously to other providers of local news, […] share its expertise and experience providing advice in training and mentoring" (2008: 62–63).

There were two further noteworthy diversions during the 2006–2016 Charter Period relating to the provision of local news – Independently Funded News Consortia (IFNC) and city-based local television – demonstrating that it was still seen as an issue to be solved, no matter how much local newspaper owners argued to the contrary. The IFNC was an initiative proposed towards the end of the Labour government in 2009. Ofcom wanted to test whether it was viable to increase plurality in local news provision via "independently funded consortia to provide an alternative source of news to the BBC in the devolved nations and English regions" (Ofcom 2009: 9). The rationale was partly based on the potential impact on media plurality following the 2008 economic crash. Ofcom was worried about how the already-depleted local newspaper industry would emerge on the other side of the recession:

> Some property and display advertising may return, and newspaper owners may be able to make further savings; however operating margins are likely to be much reduced, and some currently unprofitable titles could continue to lose money for some time.
>
> (Ofcom 2009: 5)

The proposed IFNC would be supported by public funds and were envisaged as replacing ITV's regional news services (something ITV were keen on dropping) with:

> Consortia [that] could include those with new media expertise, players from the film industry who are accustomed to bidding for public funds, businesses with brands that have a proven resonance with the target audience, commercial broadcasters, charities and other cultural institutions.
>
> (Ofcom 2009: 55)

However, despite consortia (which included some newspaper groups) making successful bids for schemes in the north-east of England, Wales, and Scotland, the incoming Conservative–Liberal Democrat coalition government of 2010 scrapped the scheme, instead favouring city-based local television services that would be standalone channels offering some local news amongst other programming. Local TV launched in 2011 but further rollout was scrapped in 2018, with Ofcom regarding it as not financially viable to fund the infrastructure changes required for any further stations to be able to start up (BBC 2018). Having been funded via a top slice of the BBC Licence fee (effectively by the BBC being obliged to acquire video content from the local stations), by 2015, MPs had dismissed the value of this version of local TV: "these services do not appear to have had any significant impact among audiences nor have they made a meaningful contribution to the provision of local news and content and as such their viability remains in doubt" (House of Commons Culture and Committee 2015: 62). The 34 city TV stations still in operation as of 2021 were mostly owned by just two large companies, often serving up as little as 10 minutes of local news a day from production bases outside of the localities they serve (Ofcom 2019).

Cementing local news partnerships

The period ahead of the 2016 BBC Charter renewal seemed marked by a continuation of the mostly frosty relationship between the state broadcaster and the regional press. This time it was the BBC's local online news presence rather than its local television news provision that the news industry had in its sights, arguing that its growth and its localness represented a threat to local newspapers. Newspaper owners and editors were able to draw on support for this view from the Conservative government, with Theresa May (then Home Secretary) telling the Society of Editor's annual conference in 2013 that:

> Local newspapers are having a particularly hard time. That has partly been the result of the BBC's dominant position on the internet, and its ability to subsidise the provision of internet news using the licence fee. This makes it enormously difficult for local newspapers to compete. If the BBC can, as they do, provide all the locally significant news, what is left to motivate the local reader to buy a paper?
>
> (May 2013)

But the nature of the relationship was changing. In 2014, James Harding, the then BBC Director of News and Current Affairs, declared that the BBC would "like to help" (Harding 2014) the local newspaper industry and had already set up tentative pilot initiatives in Leeds and Birmingham that drew on its template from the 2008 assessment of Local Video Proposals (BBC 2008). The pilots would:

> see [in Leeds] how the BBC online can make more of local newspapers' stories and digital content of local newspapers to our audiences online [and, in Birmingham] make available BBC video and audio content available to local newspaper websites, extending both our reach as well as their dwell time and comprehensive coverage of particular stories.
>
> (Harding 2014)

Aspects of the pilot initiatives were rolled out wider with the BBC linking to local news sites via its Local Live news feed and also reaching out to community hyperlocal websites (Holdsworth 2015). The News Media Association, representing the regional press, pushed the BBC on the detail of its plans, making suggestions on how linking should work and how the BBC could be clearer in: "attribution of other news brands where relevant to how the BBC has sourced or checked a story" (Oliver & Ohlbaum Associates Ltd 2015: 60). It also mooted "co-funding mutual ventures in functional areas of reporting" (2015: 69), free access to packaged BBC news material for reuse by the local press, and, conversely, "consider ways by which it's [the BBC's] sourcing of news is more open to paying for contributions from the wider news sector" (ibid.; BBC 2017).

LDRS would be the mechanism for the "mutual venture" and the initial tranche of funding for 145 reporters was largely split between the large newspaper groups (BBC 2017). Community media organisations have had limited success in drawing on resources from the Local News Partnership with a recognition from the BBC that contracts for LDRS reporters are skewed towards "large, print, pan-UK suppliers" (2020: 9). The Centre for Community Journalism has acted as a broker for the community media sector and in the 2017 LDRS allocation helped four independent publishers to secure contracts as well as ensuring access to the News Hub service for community news providers (Centre for Community Journalism 2017: 6). Community publishers were more successful in the 2021 allocation with a London-based publisher of three community newspapers, along with seven other independent publishers, securing reporters. For the moment, the scheme remains funded via the BBC licence fee at £8 million per year until the end of the current Charter Period (2027). The initial plans to expand the scheme further, by using revenues from partner advertising on content syndicated from the News Hub service, proved impossible, as the BBC would not allow advertising to be incorporated into its videos (as pre- or post-roll) (BBC 2020: 9). The government's response to the Cairncross recommendation of further public support for the LDRS element has seen the issue batted back to the BBC (Department for Digital, Culture, Media and Sport 2020) that so far has suggested that it may set up a: "Local Democracy Foundation – employing independent reporters to cover what really matters to local communities" (Hall 2019). It seems nobody has a clear sense of where the money would come from after the current Charter Period ends, with John Whittingdale, the Minister for Media and Data stating: "we will be looking in every possible quarter to see if we can find people who might be willing to contribute to it" (Select Committee on Communications and Digital 2020: Q172).

Critical regionalism

This introduction has offered a critical account of the recent ups and downs in the relationship between the BBC and the newspaper industry.

To some extent a happy compromise seems to have been achieved: local newspapers across the UK have been given the resources to cover important matters related to the functioning of local democracy; BBC-produced regional television news is available for reuse by community and commercial local media partners; and local journalists are being upskilled in innovative content creation approaches. During the period outlined earlier, the BBC has had to be attentive to their role in the local news market, negotiating with a news industry that has repeatedly asked for it to stay off their local patch. Largely, politicians from all sides have supported this view, seeking solutions that have allowed the legacy news industry recourse to public funds. Effectively, local public interest journalism has become de-commercialised and as Christopher Ali has pointed out, the communications regulator has found itself caught in the middle, with Ofcom: "attempting to regulate an industry through the lightest means possible in an era of neoliberalization and globalisation, all the while stressing the normative importance of local news and information" (Ali 2017: 114).

Ali has usefully argued for what he calls a "critical regionalism" (Ali 2017: 48) approach to studies of policy and practice in local media. That is, a way of thinking beyond reductive notions of the local in order to "identify, examine, and celebrate alternatives to the status quo" (ibid.). As we have seen previously, "local" and "community" are certainly slippery terms, in turn romanticised (or "fetishized" as Ali argues 2017: 441) as much by those seeking to attract investment or subsidy for commercial news ventures, as those in community media who situate themselves as an authentic local voice, there to reinforce and protect idealised notions of community life (Harte et al. 2018: 195). Yet a critical regionalism approach allows us to see beyond the jockeying for position of the various actors and identify the moments that open up for regulators to seize "the opportunity to rethink their concepts and thereby engage in a more complex way with the substance of the local" (Ali 2017: 48). We may be in one of those moments.

About this book

This book responds in part to Karin Wahl-Jorgensen's call for more research into local and community journalism "to better understand not just what is lost – including local information and community-building, but also how it can be regained" (Wahl-Jorgensen 2019: 165). The chapters collected in this book look at, and beyond, the mainstream, offering insights into how news organisations are trying to get audiences to continue to engage with valuable public service journalism and how shifting policies, practices, and technologies are impacting that. Scholars, practitioners, and campaigners offer original research and personal reflections on the conditions needed for developing and sustaining models for economically viable, participatory local news services. While we look at wider policy and practice issues – the absence of local news in emerging news deserts, the implementation of direct government support, the datafication and centralisation of local news production – we also look in detail at the possibilities that are opening up for independent news producers, and in that, the potential for an increased plurality in local news provision.

References

Abernathy, P.M. (2020) *News deserts and ghost newspapers: will local news survive.* Center for Innovation and Sustainability in Local Media, School of Media and Journalism, University of North Carolina at Chapel Hill. Available at: www.usnewsdeserts.com/wp-content/uploads/2020/06/2020_News_Deserts_and_Ghost_Newspapers. pdf.

Ali, C. (2017) *Media localism: the policies of place.* Urbana: University of Illinois Press.

Ali, C., Schmidt T.R., Radcliffe D., et al. (2019) The digital life of small market newspapers. *Digital Journalism* 7(7): 886–909.

Anderson, C.W. (2011) Between creative and quantified audiences: web metrics and changing patterns of newswork in local US newsrooms. *Journalism* 12(5): 550–566.

BBC. (2004) *Building public value: renewing the BBC for a digital world.* London: BBC.

BBC. (2005) *Mark Thompson announces plans for local TV pilot in West Midlands.* Available at: www.bbc.co.uk/pressoffice/pressreleases/stories/2005/03_march/18/localtv.shtml (accessed 9 April 2021).

BBC. (2008) *BBC management's assessment of the public value of its local video proposals.* London: BBC.

BBC. (2017) *BBC announces media organisations which will employ Local Democracy Reporters as latest step in the Local News Partnerships.* Available at: www.bbc.co.uk/mediacentre/latestnews/2017/local-democracy-reporters (accessed 11 April 2021).

BBC. (2018) *Ofcom seeks to scrap local TV roll-out.* Available at: www.bbc.co.uk/news/technology-43837949 (accessed 6 April 2021).

BBC. (2020) *A review of the BBC Local News Partnership.* London: BBC.

Centre for Community Journalism. (2017) *Annual report.* Cardiff: Cardiff University.

Coleman, A. (2018) *Angry people in local newspapers.* London: Penguin.

Department for Digital, Culture, Media and Sport. (2019) *The Cairncross Review: a sustainable future for journalism.* London: Department for Digital, Culture, Media and Sport.

Department for Digital, Culture, Media and Sport. (2020) *Government response to the Cairncross Review: a sustainable future for journalism.* Available at: www.gov.uk/government/publications/the-cairncross-review-a-sustainable-future-for-journalism/government-response-to-the-cairncross-review-a-sustainable-future-for-journalism (accessed 21 April 2021).

Dorwick, M. (2021a) *It's doing alright isn't it. We've also got a native post which has had some hilarious responses [Twitter] 11 February 2021.* Available at: https://twitter.com/MollyLDowrick/status/1359911299786936323?s=20.

Dorwick, M. (2021b) Scenes of devastation in Stoke after wind wreaks havoc with wheelie bins. *Plymouth Live*, 11 February 2021. Available at: www.plymouthherald.co.uk/news/plymouth-news/live-stoke-wind-wheelie-bins-4993216 (accessed 23 April 2021).

Dorwick, M. (2021c) *Thank you for understanding the humour... not everyone did! [Twitter] 11 February 2021.* Available at: https://twitter.com/MollyLDowrick/status/1359904523914014724?s=20.

Edge, M. (2019) Are UK newspapers really dying? A financial analysis of newspaper publishing companies. *Journal of Media Business Studies* 16(1): 19–39.

Gulyas A., O'Hara S. and Eilenberg J. (2019) Experiencing local news online: audience practices and perceptions. *Journalism Studies* 20(13): 1846–1863.

Hall, T. (2019) *The BBC and the future of news.* Available at: www.bbc.co.uk/mediacentre/speeches/2019/tony-hall-lords (accessed 8 April 2021).

Harding, J. (2014) *James Harding – 2014 revival of local journalism conference.* Available at: www.bbc.co.uk/mediacentre/speeches/2014/james-harding-local-journalism-conference (accessed 6 April 2021).

Harte, D., Howells, R. and Williams, A. (2018) *Hyperlocal journalism: the decline of local newspapers and the rise of online community news.* London: Routledge.

Hereford Times, (2006) Local TV under fire at debate. *Hereford Times*, 13 April 2006. Available at: www.herefordtimes.com/news/732439.local-tv-under-fire-at-debate/ (accessed 20 April 2021).

Hess, K. and Waller, L. (2012) 'The Snowtown we know and love': small newspapers and heinous crimes. *Rural Society* 21(2): 116–125.

Higgerson, D. (2015) *When you look at the dictionary definition of clickbait, critics of popular content suddenly look like journalistic snobs.* Available at: https://davidhiggerson.wordpress.com/2015/09/19/when-you-look-at-the-dictionary-definition-of-clickbait-critics-of-popular-content-suddenly-become-journalistic-snobs/ (accessed 1 August 2019).

Higgerson, D. (2017) *Greggs opening drive thrus and the perception problem caused by unbundled content.* Available at: https://davidhiggerson.wordpress.com/2017/06/24/greggs-opening-drive-thrus-and-the-perception-problem-caused-by-unbundled-content/ (accessed 18 May 2018).

Higgerson, D. (2019) *How the page view will help save journalism.* Available at: https://davidhiggerson.wordpress.com/2019/01/26/how-the-page-view-will-help-save-journalism/ (accessed 26 January 2019).

Holdsworth, D. (2015) *BBC seeks views of community news websites and bloggers.* Available at: www.bbc.co.uk/blogs/aboutthebbc/entries/d148ee0f-7bc1-4db4-8170-13b13eb2faac (accessed 8 June 2016).

House of Commons Culture, Media and Sport and Committee. (2015) *Future of the BBC: fourth report of session 2014–15.* London: The Stationery Office.

House of Lords Communications and Digital Committee. (2020) *Breaking news? The future of UK journalism.* London: The Stationery Office.

Jenkins, J. and Jeronimo, P. (2021) Changing the beat? Local online newsmaking in Finland, France, Germany, Portugal, and the U.K. *Journalism Practice*: 1–18. DOI: 10.1080/17512786.2021.1913626.

Jenkins, J. and Nielsen, R.K. (2020) Preservation and evolution: local news papers as ambidextrous organizations. *Journalism* 21(4): 472–488.

Laughton, R. (2006) *The BBC's local television pilot in the West Midlands.* London: BBC.

May, T. (2013) *Speech to society of editor's annual conference.* Available at: www.maidenhead-advertiser.co.uk/news/18415/In-full--Theresa-May-s.html (accessed 27 April 2021).

Mayhew, F. (2021) *Paywalls, micropayments and donations: how regional press giants are trying to make news pay.* Available at: https://pressgazette.co.uk/paywalls-micropayments-and-donations-how-regional-press-giants-are-trying-to-make-news-pay/ (accessed 18 April 2021).

Moore, M. (2014) *Addressing the democratic deficit in local news through positive plurality. Or, why we need a UK alternative of the knight news challenge.* London: Media Standards Trust.

Newman, N., Fletcher R., Schulz A., et al. (2020) *Reuters institute digital news report 2020.* Oxford: Reuters Institute for the Study of Journalism.

Newspaper Society. (2005) *Written evidence. Select committee on the BBC charter review.* Available at: https://publications.parliament.uk/pa/ld200506/ldselect/ldbbc/128/128we41.htm. (Accessed 25 March 2021)

Ofcom. (2004) *Ofcom review of public service television broadcasting. Phase 1—is television special?* London: Ofcom.

Ofcom. (2009) *Ofcom's second public service broadcasting review.* London: Ofcom.

Ofcom. (2019) *Letter to That's Media Limited, 8 July 2019.* Available at: www.ofcom.org.uk/__data/assets/pdf_file/0027/155583/Local-TV-studio-locations.pdf (accessed 21 April 2021).

Oliver & Ohlbaum Associates Ltd. (2015) *UK news provision at the crossroads: the news market in the 21st century and the likely implications for the BBC's role.* Available at: www.newsmediauk.org/write/MediaUploads/PDF%20Docs/OandO_NMA_-_UK_news_provision_at_the_crossroads.pdf (accessed 20 January 2018).

Ponsford, D. and Mayhew, F. (2021) *Mirror publisher reach to cut 550 jobs in response to Covid-19 revenue hit.* Available at: www.pressgazette.co.uk/mirror-publisher-reach-to-cut-550-jobs-in-response-to-covid-19-revenue-hit/ (accessed 7 July 2020).

Press Gazette. (2005) Ultra-local TV puts papers in the line of fire. *Press Gazette.* Available at: https://pressgazette.co.uk/ultra-local-tv-puts-papers-in-the-line-of-fire/ (accessed 23 April 2021).

Radcliffe, D. (2020) Covid-19 has ravaged American newsrooms. Here's why that matters. *Niemen Journalism Lab*. Available at: www.niemanlab.org/2012/12/the-coming-death-of-seven-day-publication/ (accessed 23 April 2021).

Select Committee on Communications and Digital. (2020) *Corrected oral evidence: the future of journalism, Tuesday 14 July 2020, evidence session no. 20, questions 169–179*. Available at: https://committees.parliament.uk/oralevidence/708/pdf/ (accessed 25 March 2021).

Sharman, D. (2021a) *More than 4,400 bid to become regional journalists under Facebook scheme*. Available at: www.holdthefrontpage.co.uk/2019/news/more-than-4400-bid-to-become-regional-journalists-under-facebook-scheme/ (accessed 18 April 2021).

Sharman, D. (2021b) *Publisher creates 50 new journalism jobs in major digital expansion*. Available at: www.holdthefrontpage.co.uk/2021/news/publisher-creates-50-journalism-jobs-in-digital-expansion/ (accessed 4 May 2021).

Sharman, D. (2021c) *Publisher launches new digital title in regional expansion drive*. Available at: www.holdthefrontpage.co.uk/2021/news/publisher-launches-new-digital-title-in-regional-expansion-drive/ (accessed 18 April 2021).

Sharman, D. (2021d) *Six UK dailies receive Google coronavirus emergency funds*. Available at: www.holdthefrontpage.co.uk/2020/news/six-uk-dailies-receive-google-emergency-coronavirus-funds/ (accessed 18 April 2021).

Simon, F.M. and Graves L. (2019) *Pay models for online news in the US and Europe: 2019 update*. Oxford: Reuters Institute for the Study of Journalism.

Smith, P. (2009) The politics of UK television policy: BBC Charter renewal and the 'crisis' of public service broadcasting. In: Ross K. and Price S. (eds.) *Popular media and communication: essays on publics, practices and processes*. Cambridge: Cambridge Scholars Pub., pp.130–151.

Tobitt, C. (2021a) *Millions more seek out local news online during pandemic, figures show*. Available at: www.pressgazette.co.uk/millions-more-seek-out-local-news-online-during-pandemic-figures-show/ (accessed 18 April 2021).

Tobitt, C. (2021b) *Reach closes most of its newsrooms as Mail Online staff return to office this month*. Available at: https://pressgazette.co.uk/most-reach-journalists-work-home-after-covid-19-mail-online-prepares-return-newsroom/ (accessed 18 April 2021).

Tobitt, C. (2021c) *Reach full-year results: 'encouraging' digital revenue boost, hacking costs exceed £100m*. Available at: https://pressgazette.co.uk/reach-results-2020/ (accessed 18 April 2021).

Wahl-Jorgensen, K. (2019) The challenge of local news provision. *Journalism* 20(1): 163–166.

1 Local news deserts

Agnes Gulyas

Defining local news deserts

A number of contributors to the literature (e.g. Ali 2017; Anderson 2020) highlight that the field of local news and journalism is under-theorised, reflected by the absence of any agreed definition of key concepts. Notably, the "local" in local news and journalism has been interpreted varyingly; in some studies, it refers to news produced for metropolitan cities (Anderson 2013), in others, it is community news broadcast to a part of a town (Coleman 2021), yet in others, it is online hyperlocal news provision for a small community of people (Harte et al. 2019). These varied interpretations suggest though that geographical location is a key element of local news and journalism, and for some this spatial aspect is *the* defining feature (Anderson 2020). However, there is no agreement about the nature of this spatial aspect, such as size, nor to what extent and how other factors – such as social, political, or regulatory – shape understandings of local news and journalism. Recent attempts have argued for broad definition of the local, such as Ali's critical regionalism which "forces an interrogation of localism that goes beyond place to include elements of culture, identity, and language" (Ali 2017: 107). Hess and Waller (2016) offer their geo-social model for understanding local news comprising five key concepts: geo-social, local, local habitus, community, and sense of place. Thus, while interpretations vary, there seems to be some agreement that both spatial and societal features are important in understanding local news and journalism. However, a recent review of the field (Gulyas and Baines 2020) reveals that studies tend to focus more on societal aspects when researching local news and journalism, while arguably the spatial element is under-researched.

Given the lack of consensus on key terminology, it is perhaps unsurprising that there is no agreed definition for local news deserts either. Abernathy (2018), whose Expanding News Desert project has been

DOI: 10.4324/9781003173144-2

influential in popularising the term both within academic and non-academic literature, first defined news deserts as "community without a newspaper" but later redefined them to include "communities where residents are facing significantly diminished access to the sort of important local news and information that feeds grassroots democracy" (Abernathy 2018: 97). Usher (2015) sees news deserts as "essentially an uncovered geographical area that has few or no news outlets and receives little coverage" (par 9). Similar concepts, such as media or news gaps, have also been used to describe the phenomenon. For example, Ferrier (2014) refers to media deserts, defined as a "geographic locale without access to fresh local news and information to inform and educate the public" (2). These various definitions suggest that news deserts generally refer to the lack of, or diminished availability, access or use of local news or media to a community in a geographical area. Studies on local news deserts are inherently comparative. To establish whether there is a lack or diminished availability of local news, they compare and contrast provisions in different locales, or in one locale at different time periods. In this sense, the study of local news deserts, at its core, is preoccupied with spatial inequalities regarding news provision and consumption, sometimes studied in temporal context.

Spatial inequalities, and the role of space more generally, has not featured as an important factor in news and journalism research or media studies more widely. However, other disciplinary areas have developed useful insights that could help us to understand local news deserts. In economics, spatial inequality is defined as a disparity in resources and services due to discrepancies in social and economic factors across geography (Kanbur and Venables 2005). Spatial inequality is a dimension of overall inequality, arising from considerations of interpersonal inequality in relation to access to resources and capital (ibid.). Kanbur and Venables (2005) also argue that spatial inequality is significant because it accounts for around one-third of total inequality and has a capacity to contribute to the undermining of social and political stability, especially if it aligns with political and ethnic tensions. In geography, a key question in the study of spatial inequalities, and socio-spatial organisation of places in general, is how they affect social cohesion and the capacity for a community to come together and decide on a common future (Cassiers and Kesteloot 2012).

Arguably, there are two particular insights from research on spatial inequalities in other disciplines that could benefit the study of local news deserts. First is the consideration of spatial scales, which is the geographical level at which inequality is studied. Overall, there is a tendency to focus on national and urban scales when researching spatial inequalities (Lobao et al. 2007), while "their relative obscurity along with lower interest and priority for subnational and peripheral places masks the problems of measurement and data production that are frequently at issue for small scale spatial concepts" (Tickamyer 2000: 809). Lobao et al. (2007) argue for the importance of studying the "missing middle" – the spatial scale between nation and city – because focusing on national and urban scales has led to a gap in our understanding of structures and processes at subnational levels. Second is the consideration for social justice and the purpose of studying spatial inequalities. Arguably, researching spatial inequalities should go beyond just recognising variations between different localities and aim to identify how and why spatial context contributes to inequality. Massey's (1994) concept of "power geometry" could be particularly useful here as it highlights that spatiality is both shaped by, and reproduces, power relations in society, which then implies that spatial inequalities "are both products and sources of other forms of inequality" (Tickamyer 2000: 806).

Regardless of the disciplinary approach, spatial inequalities are seen as significant because of their potential social, political, and cultural consequences. This is echoed in research on local news deserts where they are seen as a negative development that could have grave consequences for the communities affected. Most often cited implications include decline in vibrancy and engagement in local community (Ferrier 2014); less efficient, more costly, unscrutinised local government and individuals and organisations with more partisan agendas filling the vacuums (Napoli et al. 2018); decline in citizens' civic engagement (Shaker 2014); less informed citizens; and increased democratic deficit (Nielsen 2015; Rubado 2019).

Approaches to studying local news deserts

Alongside the varied interpretations, and arguably as a result of that, there have been considerable differences in the approach taken and methods applied to study local news deserts. As mentioned previously, at its core research on this topic is preoccupied with spatial inequalities and comparing availability, access, or use of local news or media between different localities and/or across time. However, there is no agreement on the precise indicators for and methodology to study local news deserts. There are four main approaches that have emerged in the literature:

> *Outlet focused*: This approach examines variations between different localities based on availability of local media outlets

on a large, usually national, scale. This approach tends to concentrate on local newspapers, justified by the historical, social, and political importance of the medium (particularly in Western democracies). As Abernathy (2018) argues "local newspapers are the best medium to provide the sort of public service journalism that shines a light on the major issues confronting communities and gives residents the information they need to solve their problems." However, some studies (e.g. Da Silva and Pimenta 2020; Lindgren and Corbett 2021) also include broadcast or online media outlets in their analysis. This approach also tends to focus on national scale aiming to identify patterns in a country which are then visualised in maps. Methodologically, projects use databases of local media availability in specified administrative geographical units (e.g. municipality, postcode area) and apply these to analyse and map spatial inequalities in local news provisions. However, databases vary in terms of level of detail, how they are maintained and the geographical unit used, thus these projects are often not comparable.

Content focused: This approach focuses on exploring variations between communities in relation to how well served they are with local news content and the robustness of local journalism. The main method is content analysis and although the approach is comparative given the more in-depth analysis, it is not carried out at national scale. For example, Napoli et al. (2018) studied 100 randomly sampled US communities as part of which they identified which ones were more at-risk of having no local news stories and of their critical information needs not being served.

Media ecology focused: Here researchers tend to explore one large or a limited number of smaller ecosystems, but in greater detail than the approaches earlier, often combining qualitative and quantitative methods and examining not just media related but different socio-economic factors. The focus is at subnational scale that allows comparison between communities within the chosen geographical area. For example, Stonbely (2021) studied local news provisions in the state of New Jersey in the US and how they correlated to various structural characteristics of municipalities identifying which communities were better and which ones were worse served. Ferrier (2014) studied variations in local news provisions in North Carolina and Rafsky (2020) explored local media ecology of New York.

Case study focused: This focus provides in-depth analysis of a selected geographical unit, often a town or a city, typically using qualitative methods. A number of studies with this approach aimed to examine changes over time in local news provisions in the selected locality and/or the impacts of these changes. For example, Harte et al. (2019) offer case study analysis of Port Talbot, Wales, while Mathews (2020) explores the impact of newspaper closure in Caroline County, Virginia.

While each approach has its strengths and weaknesses, there are some common methodological challenges to studying news deserts and spatial inequalities in relation to local news. First, findings from different studies are often difficult to compare or relate to, especially as research tends to be either scale or depth orientated, that is, either carried out at national scale or focusing on in-depth analysis of selected urban area(s). This division is exacerbated by the lack of, or limited, comprehensive data about local news provisions and consumptions in most countries. Second, there is no agreement regarding the spatial scale applied. There are significant variations in the applied geographical units. Some studies use larger state administrative units (e.g. counties, municipality), while others use smaller units (postcode), and yet others opt for organic boundaries of communities or local news outlets. Third, there is also no agreement regarding which qualities define local news outlets, which can be particularly tricky to establish in an online environment. For example, Lindgren and Corbett (2021) describe a local news outlet as a "news organization that maintains independence from those it covers, demonstrates a commitment to accuracy/transparency, and is devoted primarily to reporting and publishing timely, originally-produced news about local people, places, issues and events in a defined geographic area" (1). Others have broader definitions where traditional journalistic values and independence are less important. Fourth, there is limited use of audience and media consumption data in current research making it overall production focused. This is probably a result of a lack of comprehensive data on local news consumption and local media audiences in most countries and because historically research has tended to prioritise production and distribution aspects of local media.

Case study: spatial inequalities in local news provisions and reach in England

There have been considerable challenges facing local news media and journalism in the UK during the last 15 years, including the demise of traditional business models and closure of local newspapers, as highlighted in a number of studies (e.g. Nielsen 2015; Gulyas and Baines 2020). The sector has also experienced disruption from the introduction of new forms of, and new ways to, distribute local news (such as hyperlocal provisions and community groups on social media platforms). Amidst the turbulence, however, local news consumption remains relatively high in the UK at national aggregate levels. While the readership of printed local newspapers has declined, local news consumption online has expanded significantly. Data from 2020 reveal that 40.6 million (75 per cent) of UK adults read local media in print and digital (Local Media Works 2020). Precisely, 17 per cent predominantly access local news via social media platforms (Ofcom 2020). The national figures, however, do not reveal variations in local news provisions and consumption, and despite an increasing number of studies of local media in recent years, we know relatively little about this variation and which communities are better or worse supplied with local news.

The preliminary case study presented here had three aims. First, it sought to map and analyse variations in local news provisions and audience reach in England. Although there are some studies (e.g. Harte et al. 2019) that provide in-depth analysis of a locality without local news provision or changes in the provision, there has been no research on spatial inequalities in relation to local news at national scale. Second, it aimed to examine potential factors that might influence variations in local news provisions and explore how spatial context contributes to inequality. This addresses the purpose of studying spatial inequalities, discussed earlier, to go beyond just recognising variations between different localities and investigate reasons and power geometry. As a pilot study, five potential factors, each of which is shown in the literature to impact on operations and availability of local media, were considered: importance of local news reach in digital formats, media ownership, emergence of hyperlocal independent providers, presence of a local court, and significance of general deprivation. Third, the study aimed to find out the extent to which local news deserts and spatial variations in local news provision and reach could be studied with publicly available datasets. This consideration sought to address the issue of comparability between studies by relying on publicly available data that could be used openly, as well as to examine compatibility of different datasets about local news provisions and potential factors that might impact their variations.

In terms of methodology, the study collated, complied, and layered five datasets in ArcGIS (Geographical Information System software), mapped and analysed emerging patterns and relationships using a GIS tool, and visualised findings in interactive maps (Gulyas 2020). A key dataset is the freely available version of the industry-based JICREG (Joint industry Currency for Regional Media Research) database from 2019. It contains a variety of indicators for local news provisions in a JICREG area, including a number of newspapers, their print, and digital audience reach, and information about the titles such as frequency of publication, method of distribution, and whether it is paid or not. Four other datasets were used that allowed the study to examine potential factors influencing variations in local news provisions: local media ownership dataset from Media Reform Coalition (2019), a list of hyperlocal provisions from the Centre for Community Journalism (2019), a dataset of local courts in England (GOV.UK 2019), and English indices of deprivation (Ministry of Housing, Communities and Local Government 2019). The latter provide a set of relative measures of deprivations for different localities across the country based on seven facets: income, employment, education, health and disability, crime, barriers to housing and services, and living environment deprivation (Ministry of Housing, Communities and Local Government 2019). The indices are seen as the most holistic and robust tool to examine inequalities as they measure multiple deprivation. In terms of scale, postcode areas were used as they provided the unit level that the different datasets could be complied and overlaid at in the GIS software. However, the JIGREG data were based on JIGREG areas (distribution areas of news outlets) which then had to be matched with postcode district area units. A limitation of using the JIGREG database was that it could only provide data for 69 per cent of postcode areas; hence, the analysis could not be conducted at truly national scale. A further limitation of the JIGREG data was that it did not contain all local news outlets in the country, only those which audited their circulation and their website tagged by Comscore (a media analytics service). Another limitation of the study relates to the list of hyperlocal provisions that was crowdsourced and thus not comprehensive. Despite these limitations, the analysis provided useful insights, from which five key findings are presented in the following sections.

Availability of local newspapers

Although the number of local titles has been declining in past decades, in the majority of postcode areas included in the study there is at least one available. Analysis of JICREG data showed that out of the 1608 postcode areas, 4.6 per cent had no local titles, 30.7 per cent had one, 31.4 per cent had two, 23.1 per cent three, and 10.2 per cent four or more. The analysis also revealed that communities in metropolitan or large urban areas were more likely to have no, or one, local newspaper. This finding contradicts those found in the US which suggests that distance from the centre of a media market results in less local news (Stonbely 2021). In addition, results also show that areas with lower numbers of newspapers tend to have lower levels of audience reach of the main title in print, indicating that in these areas not only availability but also consumption of local news are reduced.

Reach of local news

A notable trend in the UK local news sector of the last decade has been the decline of circulation and readership of printed local newspapers, as news production, distribution, and consumption patterns have changed due to digital technologies and online platforms. Results of this study echoed this trend and showed that while the average reach (percentage of adult population, monthly) of the printed version of the main title in the JICREG areas was 23 per cent, the digital reach was 42 per cent, which means that digital reach is usually higher than print reach for local news. Both digital and print audience reach vary between areas of the country; however, variations in relation to digital reach are more extensive (results showed 30 per cent standard deviation for digital and 12 per cent for print reach). Further, analysis of the relationship between digital and print reach of a main title in an area shows no clear relationship between the two. There are areas where both are low or high, and there are also areas where just one of them is low or high. This indicates that local news audiences do not automatically switch from print to online, and that local news providers have different online strategies, some more successful than others. Areas with the lowest print as well as digital reach again tended to be in parts of metropolitan and urban areas.

Media ownership

The UK's local newspaper industry is highly concentrated with five companies publishing 80 per cent of all titles (Media Reform Coalition 2019). Local newspaper ownership is concentrated in geographical clusters, which reflects the business strategies of companies to exploit regional economies of scale. Analysis of areas with one title shows that the owner of that newspaper tends to be one of the main corporate owners (90 per cent of these areas were controlled by one of the three largest players: Reach PLC, Johnston, and Newsquest). Smaller publishers, with one or few titles, do not control areas with only one newspaper. This could be the result of corporate strategies aiming for regional dominance. However, the number of titles varies in different areas across the country suggesting that corporate dominance and strategies might be an influencing, but not the determining factor, in variations in local news provisions.

Emergence of independent hyperlocal providers

It is often perceived that hyperlocals have emerged where there was a lack of mainstream local news provision (Harte et al. 2019). Analysis of locations of independent hyperlocal providers showed that the average figure for number of titles was lower in areas with a hyperlocal than in areas that did not have them (1.83 vs 2.19). However, there was only one area with no newspaper where there was a hyperlocal, although one has to bear in mind the limitation of the dataset mentioned earlier. Further analysis did not show a direct link between the presence of hyperlocal and the number of local newspapers suggesting that emergence of new independent news provision is influenced by different factors, not just availability of traditional local news outlet in an area.

Presence of a local court

Another potential factor that is perceived to influence local news provisions is the presence of a local court in an area. Indeed, results show that most areas in the study (72 out of 74) that do not have a local newspaper also do not have a local court. However, analysis revealed that there was no significant relationship ($P = 0.92$) between the presence of local court and the number of local newspapers suggesting that this is not a factor in variations in local news provisions.

Significance of general deprivation

English indices of deprivation, which measure multiple deprivation in relation to seven facets listed earlier, were applied to examine how local news provisions in the most deprived communities compared to the averages. Geographical analysis of the indices with local news provisions data revealed that 10 per cent of the most deprived areas in England were significantly less served with local news than the averages. Of the lowest decile areas of indices of deprivation included in the sample, 56.5 per cent had no or one paper, while the average for all areas was 35.3 per cent. Of the areas identified in the study as having no local papers,

28 per cent were located in the lowest decile of indices of deprivation, indicating that communities in these areas are almost three times more likely to have no local news titles.

Conclusion

This chapter has provided an overview of different interpretations, approaches, and methods applied to study local news deserts. Although there are different definitions and even terminology, local news deserts generally refer to the lack of, or diminished availability, access or use of, local news or media to a community in a geographical area. In relation to the purpose of studying local news deserts, I argue that researching spatial inequalities should go beyond just recognising variations between different localities and aim to identify how and why spatial context contributes to inequality and links to existing socio-economic inequalities. This overview, however, has demonstrated that studying local news deserts is complex. Depending on the approach taken, it requires different datasets that often do not use compatible measurements. Other challenges identified in the chapter are comparability between different studies on local news deserts, the division between scale versus in-depth studies, variations in spatial scales applied in the different research, as well as in definitions of local news outlets.

The chapter has presented an analysis of local news deserts in England, which is the first study examining spatial inequalities in relation to local news at national scale. By compiling and layering different types of datasets of local news provision and reach, the study mapped and analysed variations between different locations and how the selected factors impacted provision and reach. Results demonstrate there are spatial inequalities in relation to local news provisions and reach in England, and most deprived communities tend to have most restricted access to local news. Findings also revealed the availability of independent hyperlocal provisions and presence of a local court do not appear to have an impact on spatial inequalities in local news provisions and reach, while media ownership was found as a potential influencing factor and underlying socio-economic inequalities as significant factor. This finding echoes the tenet of Massey (1994) that spatiality and spatial inequalities are both shaped by and reproduce power relations in society. It also resonates with insights in sociology and geography literature arguing that inequalities can result in even more exclusion and they work in cycle, where location is seen as one of the main factors (Cassiers and Kesteloot 2012). An additional aim of the study was to find out to what extent spatial variations in local news provisions and reach could be studied with publicly available datasets. It was found that publicly available comprehensive data on local news provisions and consumption in the UK are limited, and I argue that there should be a concentrated effort to address this. The datasets used in this pilot study were useful to address the research aims, but led to the limitations, discussed earlier. Further research is needed to provide a more comprehensive analysis of spatial equalities in local news and the factors influencing them, and arguably more broadly, we also need more consideration of spatiality in news and journalism research.

References

Abernathy, P.M. (2018) *The Expanding News Desert. Center for Innovation and Sustainability in Local Media, School of Media and Journalism*, University of North Carolina: Chapel Hill, NC. Available at: www.cislm.org/wp-content/uploads/2018/10/The-Expanding-News-Desert-10_14-Web.pdf.

Ali, C. (2017) *Media Localism: The Policies of Place*, University of Illinois Press: Urbana, IL, Chicago, IL and Springfield, IL.

Anderson, C.W. (2013) *Rebuilding the News: Metropolitan Journalism in the Digital Age*, Temple University Press: Philadelphia, PA.

Anderson, C.W. (2020) Local Journalism in the United States: Its Publics, Its Problems, and Its Potentials, in: Gulyas, A. and Baines, D. (eds. by) *Routledge Companion to Local Media and Journalism*, Routledge: London and New York, NY, 141–148.

Cassiers, T. and Kesteloot, C. (2012) Socio-spatial Inequalities and Social Cohesion in European Cities, *Urban Studies* 49(9), 1909–1924.

Centre for Community Journalism. (2019) *List of Hyperlocal Provisions, Centre for Community Journalism*, Cardiff: Cardiff University. Available at: www.communityjournalism.co.uk/en/.

Coleman, J. (2021) *Digital Innovations and the Production of Local Content in Community Radio*, Routledge: London.

Da Silva, C. and Pimenta, A. (2020) Local News Deserts in Brazil: Historical and Contemporary Perspectives, in: Gulyas, A. and Baines, D. (eds. by) *Routledge Companion to Local Media and Journalism*, Routledge: London and New York, NY, 44–53.

Ferrier, M. (2014) *The Media Deserts Project: Monitoring Community News and Information Needs Using Geographic Information System Technologies*, Scripps College of Communication, report.

GOV.UK. (2019) *Find a Court or Tribunal*. Available at: www.gov.uk/find-court-tribunal.

Gulyas, A. (2020) *Mapping Local News Provisions and Reach in England*, Centre for Research on Communities and Cultures, project report. Available at: https://storymaps.arcgis.com/stories/837bd6fbe374480f86f41a9bbc34bc23.

Gulyas, A. and Baines, D. (2020) (eds. by) *Routledge Companion to Local Media and Journalism*, Routledge: London and New York, NY.

Harte, D., Howells, R. and Williams, A. (2019) *Hyperlocal Journalism: The Decline of Local Newspapers and the Rise of Online Community News*, Routledge: London and New York, NY.

Hess, K. and Waller, L. (2016) *Local Journalism in a Digital World: Theory and Practice in the Digital Age*, Palgrave Macmillan: London.

Kanbur, R. and Venables, A. (2005) Spatial Inequality and Development, *Journal of Economic Geography* 5(1), 1–2.

Lindgren, A. and Corbett, J. (2021) *The Local News Map Data, February 1, 2021*, Local News Research Project at Ryerson University's School of Journalism and the University of British Columbia's SpICE Lab (Spatial Information for Community Mapping). Available at: https://localnewsresearchproject.ca/.

Lobao, L., Hooks, G. and Tickamyer, A.R. (2007) Advancing the Sociology of Spatial Inequality, in: Lobao, L., Hooks, G. and Tickamyer, A.R. (eds. by) *The Sociology of Spatial Inequality*, State University of New York Press: Albany, NY, 1–25.

Local Media Works. (2020) *Research Insights: Facts and Figures*. Available at: www.localmediauk.org/Research-Insight/Facts-Figures.

Massey D. (1984) *Space, Place and Gender*. Cambridge: Wiley.

Mathews, N. (2020) Life in a News Desert: The Perceived Impact of a Newspaper Closure on Community Members, *Journalism*. doi:10.1177/1464884920957885.

Media Reform Coalition. (2019) *Who Owns the UK Media?*. Available at: www.mediareform.org.uk.

Ministry of Housing, Communities and Local Government. (2019) *English Indices of Deprivation 2019*. Available at: www.gov.uk/guidance/english-indices-of-deprivation-2019-mapping-resources.

Napoli, P., Weber, M., McCollough, K. and Wang, Q. (2018) *Assessing Local Journalism: News Deserts, Journalism Divides, and the Determinants of the Robustness of Local News, Report, News Measures Research Project*, Stanford: DeWitt Wallace Center for Media & Democracy.

Nielsen, R.N. (2015) (ed. by) *Local Journalism: The Decline of Newspapers and the Rise of Digital Media*, Reuters Institute for the Study of Journalism.

Ofcom. (2020) *News Consumption in the UK: 2020*, Jigsaw Research: London.

Rafsky, S. (2020) *Media Mecca or News Desert? Covering Local News in New York City*, a tow/knight report, Tow Center for Digital Journalism.

Rubado, M.E. and Jennings, J.T. (2019) Political Consequences of the Endangered Local Watchdog: Newspaper Decline and Mayoral Elections in the United States, *Urban Affairs Review* 56(5), 1327–1356.

Shaker, L. (2014) Dead Newspapers and Citizens' Civic Engagement, *Political Communication* 31(1), 131–148.

Stonbely, S. (2021) *What Makes for Robust Local News Provision?*, report, Center for Cooperative Media, Montclair State University.

Tickamyer, A. (2000) Space Matters! Spatial Inequality in Future Sociology, *Contemporary Sociology* 29(6), 805–813.

Usher, N. (2015) *Does New Jersey Have a 'Media Desert' Problem? Columbia Journalism Review*. Available at: https://www.cjr.org/analysis/new_jersey_media_desert.php. (Accessed 21 August 2021).

2 All in, all together? Government subsidy for news

Jonathan Heawood

Introduction

This chapter examines the UK Government's approach to subsidising the news industry in the period between April 2020 and March 2021, with specific reference to a publicly funded advertising campaign called *All in, all together*. As Executive Director of the Public Interest News Foundation (PINF), a charity that promotes public interest news, I was directly involved in some of the events of this period. This gives me the advantage of first-hand experience, but also means that I cannot claim to be a disinterested observer. Nonetheless, in this detailed account, I aim to provide a fair and accurate summary of the actions of the Government and other parties during this period and to evaluate this campaign against normative criteria for an effective and legitimate press subsidy.

Context

In recent years, governments around the world have launched various initiatives in support of the print and digital news industry. These initiatives – varying from tax breaks in Canada to "innovation subsidies" in Norway – make use of both direct and indirect forms of support. In 2018, the UK Government commissioned Dame Frances Cairncross to review the sustainability of high-quality journalism and to identify "where there are underlying and persistent structural market failures which might require Government intervention" (Cairncross 2019: 114–115).

Cairncross was advised by an expert panel and took evidence from stakeholders across the news industry, academia, and civil society. Following her year-long review, she identified two areas of particularly significant market failure in the provision of public interest news:

DOI: 10.4324/9781003173144-3

One is investigative and campaigning journalism, and especially investigations into abuses of power in both the public and the private sphere. Such journalism is particularly high-cost and high-risk. The second is the humdrum task of reporting on the daily activities of public institutions, particularly those at local level, such as the discussions of local councils or the proceedings in a local Magistrates' Court.

(Cairncross 2019: 17)

To address these market failures, Cairncross recommended that the Government should establish a new Institute for Public Interest News (IPIN), to allocate public funding to news publishers, both to subsidise uncommercial forms of public interest journalism and to help the industry make the transition from print to digital publishing models. Cairncross recommended that, to mitigate any risk of political influence, IPIN should operate at arm's length from government, with an independently appointed chair. Further, it should be funded through an endowment rather than annual grant-in-aid, which would be more vulnerable to political pressure (Cairncross: 100–102).

In its official response to Cairncross, published in January 2020, the Government categorically rejected Cairncross's recommendations for an institute and a subsidy. It gave two reasons for refusing to subsidise journalism. First, it said, "it is not for the government to define what qualifies as 'public interest' news" (DCMS 2020, para 51). In other words, to implement a subsidy, any government would need to evaluate whether individual publishers or sectors of the news publishing industry were worthy of support, and this Government did not want to do that. Second, it said: "even an arm's length relationship risks perceptions of inappropriate government interference with the press" (ibid.). The Government did not provide further evidence in support of these claims or respond to Cairncross's proposals to mitigate the risk of "government interference" by ensuring the appointment of an independent chair or funding IPIN through an endowment. The position was clear: the Government recognised the crisis in public interest news but did not intend to address this crisis through any kind of subsidy.

So, it was a surprise when, only three months later, the Government launched a dedicated package of financial support for the press, in the form of the *All in, all together* public advertising campaign. How can we explain the Government's apparent *volte-face*? Was this advertising campaign a subsidy or not? If it was a subsidy, how did the Government mitigate the risk of political interference in the press? And what can we take from this experience to inform the development of any future subsidy?

All in, all together

In late March 2020, the UK news industry began to raise concerns about the impact of the COVID-19 pandemic on its economic viability. The News Media Association (NMA), which represents large national and regional newspaper publishers, described the news industry as the "fourth emergency service," and called for "immediate financial and operational support for all UK news publishers, national, regional and local" (News Media Association 2020). The NMA made six recommendations, two of which related to potential subsidies:

- Committing to divert Government media spend to newspapers (online and print, national, and local) to ensure key public information messages are communicated to readers through an immediate and sustained advertising campaign.
- Opening up additional £25,000 grants to smaller local news providers and creating a journalist support package by introducing a direct per capita payment to companies currently employing news journalists. (News Media Association 2020).

The National Union of Journalists (NUJ) endorsed the NMA's calls for a direct subsidy, with the important caveat that "the government should link any financial relief for media companies to guarantees on existing staffing levels" (National Union of Journalists 2020). In other words, any subsidy should be available only to companies that promised not to cut jobs.

The Independent and Community News Network (ICNN) highlighted the predicament facing independent and community-led news organisations in particular. ICNN and IMPRESS (the independent press regulator for the UK, recognised by the Press Recognition Panel) collectively represent more than 200 independent news publications, including community-led news organisations, local newspapers, investigative non-profits, and special-interest publications. At the outset of the pandemic, ICNN and the PINF surveyed this sector (Public Interest News Foundation 2020). They found that these publishers reach at least 14.9 million unique website visitors every month and circulate 427,000 printed copies of their publications, and that 75 per cent were afraid that they might be forced to close as a result of the lockdown (ibid.). These independent publishers are not represented by the NMA, and in an open letter published on 25 March 2020, Emma Meese, Director of ICNN, said that they should not be "left out of any deals made between the Government and organisations under the umbrella of the NMA" (Meese 2020).

> Many of our members are the only news publishers in their areas, some covering entire counties and cities. If these publishers are forced to close, the UK will be left with many more news black holes which we will struggle to fill again. We have stats that prove, even in areas with lots of local press, some of our members have the most engaged audiences.
>
> (Meese 2020)

Enders Analysis, an independent media consultancy that provided research for the Cairncross Review, supported ICNN's argument that independent and community-led publishers should be supported alongside their larger, corporate counterparts. Enders also echoed the NMA's call for the Government to commit its advertising budget to the news industry and said that "critical journalist salaries" should be paid by the Government (Enders 2020).

Thus, the NMA, NUJ, ICNN, and Enders all agreed on the need for immediate financial support for the news industry but differed on significant points of detail. The NMA and Enders called for government advertising to be directed towards news publishers, and for a direct subsidy in the form of grants for journalists' salaries. The NUJ and ICNN endorsed these calls but asserted that any payments should be conditional on guarantees of staffing levels (NUJ) and that all publishers should be supported, regardless of size (ICNN).

The Government did not respond publicly to any of these proposals. However, on 17 April 2020, the new government advertising campaign was launched. *All in, all together* consisted of a "cover wrap" (an advertisement that mimics the front and back page of the newspaper) containing public health information on COVID-19 with "hundreds of titles" (Newsworks 2020) carrying the campaign. The campaign was announced simultaneously by the NMA and Newsworks, a body that coordinates national and regional publishers' dealings with the advertising industry. In its statement, Newsworks explained that it had "led the industry's unified response to the government's brief," and that the campaign represented an "advertising partnership between the government and the newspaper industry" (Newsworks 2020). The Newsworks statement included an endorsement from the Minister for the Cabinet Office, Michael Gove, who said that newspapers "are the lifeblood of our communities" and that with "this campaign we are both saving lives by providing essential information to the public, and supporting cherished local institutions" (Newsworks 2020). The Government's own announcement of the campaign came two weeks later, on 30 April 2020, when the Treasury said that it intended to spend up to £35 million "in support of the print newspaper industry [...] to ensure the whole UK is aware of the latest government guidance and advice" (HM Treasury 2020).

Two things were apparent from these announcements. First, the Government was collaborating on the *All in, all together* campaign with the NMA and Newsworks, two bodies that represent only part of the news publishing industry and have no constitutional commitment to the wider public interest. Second, although Newsworks said that it had responded to "the government's brief" for this "advertising partnership" (Newsworks 2020), the Government had not published any brief and did not subsequently release details of any brief. Independent publishers and organisations such as ICNN and PINF had not been made aware of any brief and were not given any guidance about how independent publishers might benefit from this support for "cherished local institutions" (ibid.).

As Executive Director of PINF, I coordinated an immediate letter to the Minister for Media, Rt Hon John Whittingdale MP, which was co-signed by stakeholders, including Emma Meese of ICNN, Michelle Stanistreet, General Secretary of the NUJ, Dame Frances Cairncross, author of the Cairncross Review, and a number of media academics (Heawood 2020a). The letter pointed out that, according to the ICNN/ PINF survey of the sector (Public Interest News Foundation 2020), more than 60 per cent of independent publishers were going beyond traditional journalism in their response to the COVID-19 crisis. They were not only publishing news and information about the crisis but were also providing direct support to vulnerable citizens, organising online events, coordinating volunteers, and working with local businesses to provide information about home deliveries. We noted that by excluding these independent publishers from the *All in, all together* campaign, the Government was failing to support their provision of essential information to their readers. We therefore urged the Government to reconsider its decision to work exclusively with Newsworks and the NMA on the campaign.

On 27 April, Mohammad Yasin, Labour MP for Bedford, used an oral question in the House of Commons to ask Mr Whittingdale what support the Government was providing during the pandemic to local and regional news organisations (Hansard HC Deb 2020, col 106).

Whittingdale replied, saying that the Government had "put in place an unprecedented financial package to provide support to all businesses and [had] taken a number of steps to provide specific support to news publishers" (ibid.). Mr Yasin followed up by asking Whittingdale whether he agreed that

> independent publishers such as the *Bedford Independent* [a member of ICNN, which had not been supported through the *All in, all together* campaign] are providing a vital service to communities across the UK, and will he meet with the independent sector representative body, the ICNN, to agree an advertising deal for the local independent press?
>
> (ibid.)

Whittingdale responded,

> I agree with the hon. Gentleman that the independent community news sector is very important and plays an essential role in continuing to provide public information alongside the NMA members in the regional and local press. The agreement that we have reached for advertising will cover 600 national, regional and local titles, which reach something like 49 million people, but I am in touch with the ICNN and we are looking to see what other measures could be put in place to support it and to see whether it could benefit from the Government's own advertising package.
>
> (ibid.)

Following this exchange, Emma Meese and I were invited to meet Whittingdale, on 6 May 2020. At this meeting, he assured us that he was sympathetic to the plight of independent publishers. He asked us to tell the sector that he was very conscious that they had not so far received much, if any, of the advertising budget; and he acknowledged that some small publishers reach audiences that no other publication is likely to reach. However, he informed us that the Department for Digital, Culture, Media and Sport was not actually responsible for the *All in, all together* campaign, and that this was in fact being run by the Cabinet Office, the department that oversees central government communications, through a media buying agency called OmniGOV. Whittingdale said that he had made the case for the independent sector to the Cabinet Office, and that he would continue to make the case; but he also encouraged us to talk directly to OmniGOV about securing support for independent publishers.

Emma Meese and I therefore attended a meeting, on 14 May, with representatives of the Cabinet Office and OmniGOV, at which we asked how independent publishers could access the *All in, all together* campaign, which appeared to favour publishers represented by the NMA and its sister body, Newsworks (Byline Investigates 2020).[1] A representative of OmniGOV told us that, to access the campaign, we should in fact talk to the NMA and Newsworks. A week later, a Cabinet Office official emailed telling us to "continue discussion with NMA and Newsworks to progress integration into the alliance" (Cabinet Office official 2020a). We asked why small publishers should be obliged to appeal to private bodies to gain access to public funds. He simply repeated: "NMA/ Newsworks: as […] outlined during our call, we think it would be beneficial to you and your members to be part of this alliance" (Cabinet Office official 2020b). In response to our growing concern, the official emailed a third time to reiterate that we should "engage with NMA and Newsworks […] to help with evaluation and participation" (Cabinet Office official 2020c).

In the four weeks between the launch of the campaign on 17 April, and our meeting with OmniGOV and the Cabinet Office on 14 May, the framing of the campaign began to shift. What had been heralded by the Government as a form of public support for the newspaper industry as a whole was being administered in a way that benefited only part of the industry.

Government subsidy for news

On 24 June, PINF and ICNN wrote to Whittingdale to summarise our unsatisfactory dialogue with the Cabinet Office and OmniGOV and to ask for an immediate review of the *All in, all together* campaign (Heawood 2020b). We eventually received a response to this letter on 21 September (Whittingdale 2020). Meanwhile, on 14 July, Whittingdale appeared before the House of Lords select committee on communications and digital as part of its inquiry into the future of journalism. Baroness Olly Grender asked Whittingdale about the exclusion of independent publishers from the Government's advertising campaign (Select Committee on Communications and Digital 2020: Q178). Baroness Grender summarised the situation as follows:

> Ninety-five percent of the £35 million allocated went to the larger players via the News Media Association. Some of our witnesses would argue that the very large players are squeezing the smaller independent players out of existence. Are you comfortable with

that? When we asked representatives of the bigger players why the £35 million largely went to them, they said that we should ask you. It is great that you are here today, because it would be good to hear about what level of transparency there was and what consideration was given to ensuring that more of the money was pushed towards more of the small independent organisations. Also, who decided that it should be only for print, for instance, given that there are the small digital players that might have a better reach to inform audiences, which was part of the purpose?

(ibid.: Q178)

In his answer, Whittingdale acknowledged the grounds for Grender's concern, that (in his words) the "vast majority" of these funds have been allocated to members of the NMA, which "represents most of the large publishers" (ibid.). However, he attempted to explain this by arguing that the campaign was intended "to support the government's messaging during the Covid crisis" and was not intended to "prop up newspapers" (ibid.). This account of the campaign was rather different from the Government's original description, which stated that the campaign was intended "in support of the print newspaper industry" and that it would be "a vital boost to the media industry" (HM Treasury 2020). It was also at odds with both Whittingdale's own words later in the session – when he described the campaign as a "support package" (Select Committee on Communications and Digital 2020: Q178) for news publications and acknowledged that he would have liked to support more titles – and with his earlier statement in Parliament, on 27 April, when he had said that the Government had "taken a number of steps to provide specific support to news publishers" (Hansard HC Deb 2020, col 106). Thus, the initial Government position was that the campaign had twin objectives – to subsidise the press and to promote government guidance – but Whittingdale's response to scrutiny was to backtrack on this and claim that the campaign had only one objective – to promote government guidance – and that funding the newspaper industry was of secondary importance. This had the effect of downplaying concerns about the inequitable allocation of the £35 million subsidy across the news publishing industry.

Whittingdale went on to state that the allocation of the £35 million budget was entirely decided by OmniGOV:

OmniGOV was starting from scratch. It had never had any dealings with these very small publishers, so they had to go through a process of assuring themselves that these were reputable, legitimate publishers who would get to the people we needed to reach. It is also very difficult to administer hundreds and hundreds of individual tiny contracts with very small publishers. Whereas, if you talk to Newsquest, Newsquest controls 150 titles, so you can instantly reach a lot of local communities.

(Select Committee on Communications and Digital 2020: Q178)

In short, Whittingdale said that the allocation had been made by a private company, OmniGOV: "Therefore, it was relatively easy to set up a campaign with titles that they knew about. They had done due diligence, they understood the reach" (ibid.). When PINF and ICNN asked OmniGOV to consider supporting other titles, OmniGOV simply directed us towards another body, the NMA, which exists to represent the interests of large publishers and therefore has no legitimate role in the allocation of public funds. Whittingdale did not demonstrate that any consideration was given to ensuring that the budget was pushed out to independent news publishers. Quite the opposite. He acknowledged that the vast majority of the campaign budget had been allocated to members of the NMA but said that this was simply "because the NMA represents most of the large publishers" (ibid.). He also said that it was easier to administer public funding to one large publisher, such as Newsquest, than to a large number of small publishers. Finally, Whittingdale did not explain who had made the decision that the budget should be allocated only to print-first publications, or give any grounds for this decision. Nor did he address this point in his letter of 21 September 2020, in which he finally responded to our letter of 24 June 2020. In the 21 September letter, Whittingdale stated,

All of the 600+ titles in the Press Partnership have been selected independently by our media planning and buying agency, OmniGOV, on their ability to engage with audiences at a national, regional and local level and who can be verified by our media auditors. News titles that are not audited or cannot demonstrate their circulation/readership are not included in the partnership as we would not be able to demonstrate value for money. The Press Partnership continues to welcome publications who are not currently participating and who can meet this selection criteria. I suggest that you continue to work constructively with OmniGOV and the Cabinet Office on behalf of the titles you represent.

(Whittingdale 2020)

This was the first official statement of any selection criteria for inclusion in the campaign. However, it begged further questions, not least because there is no universally recognised measure of news publications' "ability to engage with audiences" (ibid.). In the past, most national, regional, and local newspapers were audited by the Audience of Bureau Circulation (ABC), which provided a standard measure of print circulation. However, many newspaper publishers have taken their titles out of the ABC framework in recent years. Moreover, digital readership is harder to calculate than print readership, given the complex digital publishing ecosystem, where some news stories are widely shared via social media platforms, which divorce these stories from their originating publisher. OmniGOV has not published its criteria for selecting publishers to participate in the *All in, all together* campaign.

After months of attempts to engage with DCMS, the Cabinet Office and OmniGOV, only one ICNN member publication, *The Wokingham Paper*, was ultimately selected to participate in the *All in, all together* campaign, or in any of the public advertising campaigns which followed – "Hands, Face, Space," "Stay Home," and "Check, Change, Go" (the latter related to the UK's departure from the European Union). The situation was different in Scotland, where the Scottish Government appointed a different agency, Republic of Media, to buy advertising on its behalf, and where eight ICNN member publications were selected to participate in the first round of public health advertising (Abbott 2021). Seven of these publications were also selected to participate in two further campaigns, "Protection Levels" and "FACTS."

Conclusion – lessons to be learnt

Whether by accident or design, the UK Government's support for the UK press during the COVID-19 crisis had the effect of favouring a certain group of publishers and disfavouring others. The Government worked closely with two private bodies, the NMA and Newsworks, while hindering attempts by other bodies to engage with the process. At the same time, by providing a subsidy in the form of advertising, the Government required news publications to carry messages that promoted government policy. In these fundamental ways, the *All in, all together* campaign sets a troubling precedent for any future subsidy of journalism. What lessons can we learn from this experience?

First, it is important to recognise that any form of subsidy – whether it takes the form of direct funding or indirect financial support via tax relief, advertising or negotiation rights with social media platforms (as in the Australian news bargaining code) – will require some degree of qualitative decision-making. At some point in the process, either parliament and/or a decision-making body will need to decide which publishers should benefit from any scheme. It would be preferable to ensure that this evaluation takes place in the light of day, through parliamentary debate and/or through public consultation on the remit of a body that is independent of political considerations. Second, therefore, the Government must set criteria that are aligned with the public interest. These criteria must be properly debated in public and in parliament. The Cairncross Review (2019) would be an obvious starting point for determining these criteria. Cairncross emphasised the need to support local journalism, investigative journalism and the industry's transition to digital. These priorities could be translated into clear criteria for selecting which news organisations to support, just as, for example, Arts Council England translates high-level public priorities into clear criteria for selecting which arts organisations to support.

Third, the use of government advertising as a subsidy poses particular challenges. In fact, there is a fundamental conflict of interests for any government which uses advertising to deliver a subsidy. As an advertiser, the government is under a duty to the taxpayer to achieve value for money. It must secure the most effective advertising at the lowest cost. This means using quantitative criteria such as audience reach and engagement, which are not necessarily synonymous with public interest journalism. The publications with the greatest reach may not provide a significant amount of public interest journalism and may not even require a subsidy. Furthermore, when government advertising takes the form of paid-for content, which blurs the distinction between advertising and editorial content, this may give rise to the public perception that the government is essentially buying favourable coverage from the press. For these reasons, any press subsidy in the form of advertising is far from ideal. Fourth, if public funds are used to subsidise journalism, then these funds must be removed as far as possible from short-term political considerations, both to ensure stability and certainty of funding and to mitigate the risk of political interference. An endowment, as suggested by Cairncross, is an obvious model, as it would give a funding body the confidence to operate without worrying whether the government was likely to reduce or cancel its budget.

Finally, any organisation delivering a subsidy should be accountable to the public. There are many examples in the UK of institutions that are operationally independent of government but accountable to parliament. These include the Charity Commission, Arts Council England, and the Press Recognition Panel. An institute of the kind recommended by Cairncross could be required to report annually on its decisions and the impact of those decisions. Similar conditions might be imposed on another body – if, for example, the government chose to endow an independent charity with funds to support public interest journalism in perpetuity. Through the *All in, all together* campaign, the UK Government has at least recognised the need to intervene in support of news publishing. However, the design and delivery of this intervention has been seriously flawed. It is to be hoped that future initiatives will improve on this experience.

Note

1 The summary of this meeting and subsequent exchanges with OmniGOV and the Cabinet Office is drawn from a letter that Emma Meese and the author sent to the House of Lords Communications and Digital Committee on 17 July 2020, and which is published on the Committee's website: https://committees.parliament.uk/writtenevidence/8973/html/.

References

Abbott, M. (2021) *Email to Jonathan Heawood*, 18 February 2021.

Byline Investigates. (2020) *£35m Covid Cash Fund Dominated by Big Media While Small Publishers Struggle.* Available at: https://bylineinvestigates.com/2020/06/03/exclusive-35m-covid-cash-fund-dominated-by-big-media-while-small-publishers-struggle/. (Accessed 22 March 2021).

Cabinet Office official. (2020a) *Email to Emma Meese and Jonathan Heawood*, 21 May 2020.

Cabinet Office official. (2020b) *Email to Emma Meese and Jonathan Heawood*, 26 May 2020.

Cabinet Office official. (2020c) *Email to Emma Meese and Jonathan Heawood*, 28 May 2020.

Cairncross, F. (2019) *The Cairncross Review: A Sustainable Future for Journalism.* London: DCMS.

DCMS. (2020) *Government Response to the Cairncross Review: A Sustainable Future for Journalism.* Available at: www.gov.uk/government/publications/the-cairncross-review-a-sustainable-future-for-journalism/government-response-to-the-cairncross-review-a-sustainable-future-for-journalism. (Accessed 6 March 2021).

Enders. (2020) *Enders Analysis Calls for Government Support for News and Magazine Media.* Available at: www.endersanalysis.com/sites/default/files/uploaded-docs/Enders%20Analysis%20Call%20For%20Government%20Support%20for%20News%20&%20Magazine%20Media.pdf. (Accessed 6 March 2021).

Hansard HC Deb. (2020). Vol 675 col 106. Available at: https://hansard.parliament.uk/Commons/2020-04-27/debates/824B1FA1-5616-42D1-B6D8-2AE0BC5C6E3C/DigitalCultureMediaAndSport. (Accessed 25 March 2021).

Heawood, J. (2020a) *Letter to Rt Hon John Whittingdale MP, Minister for Media*, 17 April 2020. Available at: www.saveindependentnews.org.uk/public-health-advertising. (Accessed 22 March 2021).

Heawood, J. (2020b) *Letter to Rt Hon John Whittingdale MP, Minister for Media*, 24 June 2020.

HM Treasury. (2020) *VAT Scrapped on e-Publications*. Available at: www.gov.uk/government/news/vat-scrapped-on-e-publications. (Accessed 20 March 2021).

Meese, E. (2020) *An Open Letter Calling for Support of ICNN Members in This Time of Global Crisis*. Available at: www.communityjournalism.co.uk/an-open-letter-calling-for-support-of-icnn-members-in-this-time-of-global-crisis/. (Accessed 6 March 2021).

National Union of Journalists. (2020) *NUJ Recommendations for Industry & Society in Response to the Coronavirus*. Available at: www.nuj.org.uk/resource/nuj-recommendations-for-industry-and-society-in-response-to-the.html. (Accessed 6 March 2021).

News Media Association. (2020) *NMA Calls for Government Support for "Fourth Emergency Service" News Media Sector During the Coronavirus Crisis*. Available at: www.newsmediauk.org/Latest/nma-government-support-for-fourth-emergency-service-news-media-sector-during-the-coronavirus-crisis. (Accessed 6 March 2021).

Newsworks. (2020) *All in, All Together*. Available at: www.newsworks.org.uk/%2fnews-and-opinion/all-in-all-together-release. (Accessed 20 March 2021).

Public Interest News Foundation. (2020) *Three Quarters of Independent News Providers in UK at Risk of Closure Due to Covid-19*. Available at: www.publicinterestnews.org.uk/post/research-three-quarters-of-independent-news-providers-in-the-uk-at-risk-of-closure-due-to-covid-19. (Accessed 20 March 2021).

Select Committee on Communications and Digital. (2020) *Corrected oral Evidence: The Future of Journalism, Tuesday 14 July 2020, Evidence Session No. 20, Questions 169–179*. Available at: https://committees.parliament.uk/oralevidence/708/pdf/. (Accessed 25 March 2021).

Whittingdale, J. (2020). *Letter to Jonathan Heawood*, 21 September 2020.

3 British community journalism's response to the COVID-19 pandemic

Karin Wahl-Jorgensen, Iñaki Garcia-Blanco, and Julia Boelle

Background: the fragility of community journalism

Even at the best of times, community journalism is widely recognised as a precarious sector (Wahl-Jorgensen 2021). The financing of outlets is frequently uncertain, and their existence is under continuous threat. As Van Kerkhoven and Bakker (2014: 297) pointed out, community news organisations are characterised by "a high degree of entry and exit and they require a heavy reliance on volunteer work and individual entrepreneurship." In their study of Dutch hyperlocal sites, they found that securing financial sustainability poses major challenges to these news organisations. Many UK community journalism outlets report a revenue of under £25,000 per year, with several turning over less than £100 a month, and just a few turn over more than £250,000 per year (Wahl-Jorgensen, 2020; see also further discussion below). In the vast majority of cases, they are run by a single person, who serves as the editor and sole reporter, as well as being responsible for managing the commercial operations of the outlet.

However, like other enterprising businesses, they are agile and flexible because of their small size, their low operational costs, and the commitment and personal investment of their workforce. They can, therefore, innovate rapidly and change their ways of working, which is a particular advantage at times of crisis. Nonetheless, the community journalism sector is facing existential threat due to the COVID-19 pandemic. More than 2,000 staff members across the UK press have temporarily lost their jobs as a result of the pandemic, and a third of industry professionals fear severe financial impact, leading to bankruptcy or insolvency (Mayhew and Turvill 2020; Tobitt 2020c). The media industry has seen a significant drop-off in advertising income, which is likely to continue in the context of the pandemic's longer term impact on corporate and public advertising budgets. For local and

DOI: 10.4324/9781003173144-4

regional newspapers, the pandemic has represented a dramatic hit to circulation, with regional daily circulation dropping by 18% in the last quarter of 2020 (Tobitt and Majid 2021). The community news sector has been identified as particularly vulnerable. At the outset of the pandemic, three-quarters of publications believed they were at risk of temporary or permanent closure due to the financial fallout (Tobitt 2020a).

At the same time, the coronavirus pandemic has represented a moment of vindication for local news, with significant increases in online audiences (Olsen et al. 2020). For example, local news sites in the UK added 2.2 million additional visitors in June 2020, compared to January of the same year (Tobbitt 2020b). The importance of local news has not gone unnoticed. As Finneman and Thomas (2021) have noted, metajournalistic discourses around the pandemic emphasised both the financial precarity of journalistic institutions and their exceptional importance to democratic societies, particularly in the context of major crises. Against this backdrop of uncertainty and change, this chapter examines how community news organisations adapted their practices as a result of the pandemic.

Methodology

The chapter is based on in-depth interviews with 57 community journalism editors, conducted between June and September 2020, and an online survey of 116 editors, carried out in March and April 2021. The research was focused on investigating the experiences and working practices of community journalists and how these have changed as a result of the coronavirus pandemic. The 57 interviewees were recruited from amongst the 123 members of the Independent Community News Network (ICNN), the main organisation representing the interests of the independent community news sector in the UK. The ICNN is hosted by the Centre for Community Journalism (C4CJ) at Cardiff University. The interviews explored the following areas: the interviewees' professional backgrounds, their route into the community journalism sector, their financial conditions, their news coverage, and their experiences during the coronavirus pandemic.[1] Interviewees were offered a £40 incentive for their participation. Interviews took place via videoconferencing software or telephone and lasted from 33 minutes up to one hour and 25 minutes (one interview was conducted via e-mail, at the request of the interviewee). The vast majority of respondents (50 out of 57) were happy to be identified and in cases where respondents wished to remain anonymous, any details that may reveal their identity have been removed for the purposes of this chapter. Interviews were transcribed and then analysed for attention to recurring themes. Interviewees represented all nations and regions of the UK, with one interviewee based in the Republic of Ireland. Of these interviewees, just 15 were women, reflecting the gender imbalance in the profession.[2] In all but a handful of cases, they were the sole individuals producing content for the outlets.

The online survey was carried out in March and April 2021. It built on measures first developed for a survey of hyperlocal publishers carried out in 2013–2014 (Williams et al. 2014). These measures were focused on assessing the democratic role of hyperlocal journalism and examining how successful and sustainable the sites are. Given our interest in the working practices of community journalists and how these have changed in the context of the coronavirus pandemic, we developed and piloted a further set of measures related to these areas. These new measures were based in part on insights gained through the interview process, which highlighted the diversity of experiences in the pandemic with respect to news production, working practices, and financial circumstances. The survey targeted a broader range of publishers: the sample included all the active contacts for publications listed on the map of 285 community news outlets hosted by the C4CJ. Contact details were found for 217 community journalism editors (some putting out more than one publication, with a total of 258 outlets). They were invited to participate via e-mail or website contact forms and were offered a £10 shopping voucher as compensation. Out of those invited, a total of 116 editors completed the survey, resulting in a response rate of 53%. Survey responses were anonymised.

Our analysis in this chapter focuses on how community journalists adapted their working practices and operations in response to the pandemic. In particular, while many experienced profound logistical and financial challenges, the crisis also reaffirmed the importance of community journalism and its centrality in local communities.

Findings: the challenges of community journalism in a pandemic

First and foremost, the pandemic resulted in a dramatic decline in advertising revenue.

Advertising is the most significant source of income for community journalism outlets, with 75% receiving at least some advertising income. More than half (51.7%) of the surveyed publications reported a decline in advertising income, compared to just 7.8% seeing an increase following on from the pandemic. Our survey showed that 13 respondents (11.2%) thought they may be forced to shut down their publications, while four (3.4%) had stopped publishing since the start of the pandemic. Although the number of outlets that have closed or are at risk of closure is smaller than predicted at the outset of the pandemic, it still vividly highlights the precarity of the sector. In reflecting on why they may need to close down their publications, some editors mentioned longer standing problems not directly related to the pandemic. These problems included burnout, the lack of a valid business model, an ageing volunteer-based workforce, a longer term decline in advertising revenue and simply being "bored." However, in several cases, the pandemic had pushed their publications over the edge, with editors commenting in our survey that the "coronavirus outbreak has hit our paper-based copy," that there is a real "danger of advertisers not returning and grants drying up," and that "the losses sustained over the past year have reduced the site's reserves to the point where further losses would be unsustainable."

While the loss of advertising revenues hit the majority of the outlets, some are funded by other means and were therefore not affected. For example, *VIEWdigital* is a social justice-focused magazine in Northern Ireland that relies on sponsorship, rather than advertising, and benefited from a large donation from a local philanthropist. Many other publications rely on volunteer labour. Mike Rawlins, who publishes the community website *MyTuriff*, based in Scotland, explicitly describes his work as "a hobby":

> So if it cost me a few quid it's cheaper than paying for a golf subscription. And that's honestly the way I look at it [...]. I could go and play golf badly. And that's gonna cost me, what, 500 pounds a year. And, well actually I quite enjoy doing that [work on the website] and I think there's a value to it.

Indeed, those doing community journalism as a "hobby" or in addition to a day job constituted a significant minority among interviewees. In our survey, which included less well-established community journalism outlets, just over two in five (41%) reported an income over £1,000 a month. However, this compares to just under a quarter (24.1%) reporting this level of income in the 2013–2014 survey (Williams et al., 2014), suggesting the growing professionalisation and viability of the sector. Just over one in four (25.9%) currently have an income more than £2,000 a month.

While volunteer labour has always been essential to the sector (e.g. Harte et al. 2018; Moore 2015), our research also suggests that a growing number of editors are now able to devote themselves to working full time. For those who do, the pandemic proved a particular financial challenge. Joe Willis, of *Richmondshire Today*, believes that as a local news provider, he "should be able to get a living from that service, just the same as the local builder, the plumber, the solicitor should." When the pandemic hit, he thought up several new enterprises, including a local dating site and a county-wide news site. To supplement his income, he also started making deliveries for a local gin distillery.

The pandemic did not just shake the financial foundations of the sector but also represented a profound challenge to distribution. For those outlets that produce print editions, many had to temporarily halt or change the format of their publications, as printing and distribution became difficult or impossible. Our survey data indicate that 39.7% of outlets produce a print edition, which suggests that a significant proportion of community journalism outlets were affected by these challenges. Of those with print editions, 63% stopped publishing during the pandemic.

While only some of the publishers saw their printers shut down shop, editors had to weigh up whether putting out a print edition was logistically and financially feasible. For many, the loss of advertising income made the print edition financially unviable. For example, Mark McGinley, who works with his wife to put out three bimonthly papers in the London suburbs of Peckham, Dulwich, and Lewisham, explained that they had suspended one issue of each of their papers after advertisers pulled out. All advertising is paid in advance, and when the full implications of the lockdown became clear, the cafes, restaurants, and pubs that provided much of their advertising revenue had been in touch to ask for postponement. McGinley was sympathetic to the predicament of the businesses, but the withdrawal of advertising also pushed him to consider his plans:

> You've got nothing to advertise, you're not open, that would be taking your money and swindling, just tell us when you're ready to advertise again. So we quickly realised you know, we should probably [...] take a break anyway.

As a result, McGinley and his partner suspended publication for one two-month cycle, returning to publication in June 2020. Other publishers continued to produce the paper in electronic format but suspended printing. Jon Dunham, of the *Hastings Independent*, was one of several editors who opted to publish a PDF version of the paper online. In one particularly harrowing case, John Baron, of the *West*

Leeds Dispatch, had been planning for years to put out a print edition, drawing on extensive contributions from volunteers in the community he had recruited and trained as citizen journalists:

> We were a week away from launching a 32-page tabloid, 5,000 copy print run, and we had to scrap that. I was absolutely, absolutely devastated. It had taken so much time and work to kind of get it to there. So COVID scuppered that all the way.

However, Baron subsequently received a €5,000 grant from the European Journalism Fund to help him get the print edition back on track and was planning to proceed with this after the end of the lockdown. Andy Vallis, of *Wells Voice*, scrapped his usual monthly print publication in May 2020 and instead put out a 12-page special in collaboration with the Wells Coronavirus Network, formed by community organisations. The network helped cover the printing costs, and Vallis was also able to secure advertising to help cover expenses. Richard Coulter (editor of both *Filton Voice* and *Portishead Voice*) also scrapped the May and June issues, but *Filton Voice* produced a community newsletter on high-quality paper instead, containing information on services, help, and support initiatives for local residents. The production costs (around £500) were covered by the newspaper, and it was distributed door to door through a volunteer network.

Beyond the logistics of print publication, the pandemic dramatically disrupted distribution models. Before the pandemic, most publications relied on boxes in shops, cafes, and local libraries for distributing free copies, but all of these sites closed down during the lockdown. This meant that editors had to think creatively about how to manage distribution.

Phil Creighton, of *Wokingham Paper*, conjured up an entirely new distribution network. This included handing out copies with food parcels given by the emergency community hub, partnering with an Indian takeaway restaurant that put a copy in with their takeaways and distributing copies through garden centres, which were the first businesses to open after the end of the first lockdown. In the case of *South Leeds Life*, the local vicar assisted by handing out hundreds of copies of the publication on his daily rounds in the community. *Broughton Spurtle*, a volunteer-run publication covering a neighbourhood in Edinburgh, was one of the papers whose usual printing facility closed down as a result of the lockdown. To continue publication, team members printed A4-sized copies of the paper at home. They then asked for permission to post them in the windows of local newsagents and also managed to gain access to council facilities. The editor of *Broughton Spurtle*, Alan McIntosh, described the process as follows:

> We purloined a key to the council's notice boards and basically hijacked them. And it's been appearing around the neighbourhood in those. Some parts of the council were supportive. Some parts of the council didn't know. And some parts of the council pretended they didn't know. It basically comes down to individuals. And there's such a kind of policy and enforcement vacuum in the council at the moment that it was quite easy just to push it through and get it done.

While most of the community journalism outlets that offer print editions circulate through public distribution points, *Wells Voice* is one of a small number of community journalism papers that is delivered door-to-door, as a way of maximising readership. However, the pandemic led to safety concerns for his delivery team:

> [One thing] I've done with the deliveries recently is offer them all masks and gloves and hand sanitizer as well, if they want them, while they're out there on the streets, just to try and keep them as safe as possible and reassure the public that we're trying to take safety precautions as well. [But] in April, four of my deliverers decided they didn't want to deliver. ... Some of them are quite elderly and didn't want to expose themselves to any risks. And so I did more deliveries again in April. And there was one person who challenged me and said that they thought it was madness to be delivering at that moment in time. But most people were really pleased that the *Voice* was still getting through.

These examples highlight the great lengths to which community journalism editors went to continue operating through the pandemic. In many cases, they saw their actions as the product of their commitment to the local community, reflective of a "civic value motivation" (see Harte et al. 2018, chapter 5). This commitment reflects the distinctive self-understanding of community journalists, which is premised on the importance of making a difference in the local community (Hanusch 2015; Wahl-Jorgensen, forthcoming). At the same time, the creativity of the editors in facing up to the challenges highlights the agility and flexibility of the sector, resulting from their small size and operational autonomy. This feature is not unique to community journalism but has been documented in other small business contexts (e.g. Sherehiy and

Karwowski 2014). As a result, they can rapidly innovate and change their ways of working. If the coronavirus pandemic represented a moment of crisis that necessitated a profound transformation of journalistic practices (e.g. Lewis 2020), the community journalists were well placed to bring about such dramatic change. At the same time, the pandemic also represented opportunities for positive transformation. As we discuss in the next section, while a minority of outlets saw financial benefits from the pandemic, the overwhelming majority experienced a significant increase in audience engagement and also changed their coverage to better support their communities.

The coronavirus pandemic as an opportunity for positive transformation

As Hess and Waller (2021) noted, local news could be viewed as an "essential service" in the pandemic with particular importance in rural and regional areas that are poorly served by major news organisations:

> In these places, local journalists are best placed to provide accessible news and information and contextualise global and national stories for their audiences; and significantly, to report how a crisis like COVID-19 is affecting their own institutions, businesses and people.
> (250)

Given the importance of locally specific information in a swiftly developing crisis, it is therefore not surprising that the majority of our interviewees reported an increase in audience figures as a result of the pandemic. Our survey also indicated several positive outcomes of the pandemic, with some respondents reporting an increase in audience figures (51.7%) and audience engagement (41.4%), new advertising accounts (21.6%), and an increase in advertising revenues (7.8%). A substantial minority have benefited from grant funding since the start of the pandemic (42.2%). Milo Perrin, of *Cornish Stuff*, was one beneficiary of an increase in audience interest during the pandemic, reporting a tripling in the number of site visits, and a resulting boost in online advertising revenue.

While many of our interviewees bemoaned the financial lack of support for their publications from the UK government, some were able to obtain grants from other bodies, including the Welsh Government, the Public Interest News Foundation, the European Journalism Fund, and local councils. Because of the small size of the operations, such grant funding frequently made a significant difference to their sustainability.

For example, Kathy Bailes, of *Isle of Thanet News*, had been working 12-hour days, seven days a week since launching her publication in 2017. She had her first weekend off since the site's launch in June 2020, after receiving a council grant to support businesses affected by the coronavirus pandemic, which enabled her to hire a former colleague to cover the local community and create content for her news site.

For many of the editors, the coronavirus pandemic represented a moment of journalistic reinvention. This was in part necessitated by the restriction on normal journalistic activities, such as face-to-face meetings, and a shift towards online work. Stephen Kingston, of *Salford Star*, reflected on his experience as follows:

> During the lockdown, you couldn't go out and talk to anybody. So it was just a question of literally putting the figures up, putting whatever stories came in on email. That was probably quite isolating. But it was also nice. I had a break. The phone stopped ringing, the emails stopped coming. It was great. Loved it.

However, beyond a shift in daily practices and routines, the pandemic also necessitated significant changes in the subject matter and style of journalism. James Cracknell, then editor of *Waltham Forest Echo*, became emotional when he described the shift in his reporting in the initial stages of the pandemic:

> I was born in 1985, so it's the biggest major world event that's happened in my lifetime. So, to be reporting on it [...] at the local level, means that at the very beginning I realised that my job was to literally give our readers information that could save their lives. I was like, bloody hell, that's quite a responsibility, because you had people stuck in their homes. People who were [...] literally unable to open their front door. But they needed that prescription picked up, they needed their food. And they needed someone to look out for them. [...] Overnight, you had thousands of people in the community who needed help. So I saw the job of, of us, as a local newspaper, to give them the information they needed so that they could get the help they needed. So, the front pages that we did right at the beginning, were unlike any journalism I've done before [...] Those stories we were writing in the beginning [were about] how can I give people the information they need that could save their lives.

Reflecting this shift, *Waltham Forest Echo* began to publish the details of local support services, including phone numbers for mutual aid groups, food banks, and advice lines for the elderly. Cracknell was just one of many interviewees who dramatically changed their reporting as a result of the pandemic. While 52.6% of the editors we surveyed agreed that their content had changed, our interviews shed light on the kinds of innovations that editors introduced. So, for example, Chris Titley of *YorkMix* launched a live blog for the first time in the publication's history to capture breaking news. Francesca Evans, of *Lyme Online*, opened a new tab on the site dedicated to news about coronavirus, "so people click on that rapidly to find all the latest news about how it was affecting our community." The pandemic also facilitated experiments with new platforms for disseminating news and enhancing audience engagement. Ben Black, of *Cwmbran Life*, started Facebook Live broadcasts towards the end of the first lockdown:

> I went around to five of the shops. A hardware store, a laundrette, the chip shop, the cafe and the beauty parlour. I spoke to them and said, look, do you want to take part in a Facebook Live video just about […] re-opening, and working safely. And then I got my phone out, we did a 14-minute Facebook Live video from shop to shop. […] It had thousands of views […]. Created a lot of comments.

In talking about the shift in reporting practice, editors frequently mentioned the responsibility to boost the spirits of their community, in line with an understanding of their role as community advocates and promoters (Hanusch, 2015; Wahl-Jorgensen, forthcoming). As a result, many prioritised "good news" stories (e.g. McIntyre, 2016). So, for example, Dawn Robinson-Walsh, of *Bude and Beyond*, reflected on the importance of being "the voice of calm and reason at a time of panic and concern" and showing "the nice stories that came out of it." She mentioned reporting on the many new local groups set up to help local individuals: "Very quickly, the Bude community geared up to help those who were stuck in their homes, who were isolated, who couldn't even go shopping for themselves." This suggests that, in line with community journalists' emphasis on serving the community, their coverage also sought to reflect "social cohesion and cooperation" (Gieber 1955, cited in McIntyre 2016: 224).

Conclusion

Our research has shown that the coronavirus pandemic represented a transformative moment for community journalism in the UK. On the one hand, the pandemic highlighted the fragility and precarity of the sector, with many outlets suffering dramatic declines in their advertising revenues and significant operational challenges in terms of reporting, printing, and distribution. On the other hand, the crisis also called attention to the importance of local news, with publications transforming their coverage "to literally give our readers information that could save their lives" (James Cracknell, *Waltham Forest Echo*). Community journalism editors changed both the content and the style of their reporting, often making innovative use of social media technologies. While all emphasised the need to provide relevant and timely information to their communities, many also saw it as their responsibility to boost the spirits of the community by sharing "good news stories."

Across the board, the pandemic emphasised the vital role of the sector in fostering community cohesion. Community journalism outlets were able to rapidly innovate because of their small size and flexibility. But this also makes them vulnerable to sudden changes and demonstrates the need to ensure robust support. Any consideration of the future of community journalism should therefore be informed by the insight that news production can no longer be driven purely by profit motives. Instead, visions of the future of community journalism must be informed by the idea of journalism as a public good vital to a democratic society (see also Olsen et al. 2020).

Notes

1 The research received funding from the British Academy COVID-19 grants programme. Interviews were carried out by all three authors.
2 It is unclear why community journalism is so male-dominated. In our survey, 23.5% of respondents identified as women. Some of the women we interviewed reflected on their gendered experience, with two of them describing making a deliberate choice to pursue community journalism because they saw it as a family-friendly occupation which allowed them greater flexibility to juggle care-related responsibilities (Una Murphy of *VIEWdigital* and one interviewee who wished to remain anonymous).

References

Finneman, T., and Thomas, R.J. (2021) "Our company is in survival mode": metajournalistic discourse on COVID-19's impact on US community newspapers. *Journalism Practice*, DOI: 10.1080/17512786.2021.1888149, 1–19.

Gieber, W. (1955) Do newspapers overplay "negative" news? *Journalism & Mass Communication Quarterly*, 32, 311–318.

Hanusch, F. (2015) A different breed altogether? Distinctions between local and metropolitan journalism cultures. *Journalism Studies*, 16(6), 816–833.

Harte, D., Howells, R., and Williams, A. (2018) *Hyperlocal journalism: the decline of local newspapers and the rise of online community news.* London: Routledge.

Hess, K., and Waller, L.J. (2021) Local newspapers and coronavirus: conceptualising connections, comparisons and cures. *Media International Australia*, 178(1) 21–35.

Lewis, S.C. (2020) The objects and objectives of journalism research during the coronavirus pandemic and beyond. *Digital Journalism*, 8(5), 681–689.

Mayhew, F., and Turvill, M. (2020) More than 2,000 newspaper jobs hit as hundreds of publications across UK face Covid-19 cuts. *Press Gazette*, April 16, www.pressgazette.co.uk/more-than-2000-newspaper-jobs-hit-as-hundreds-of-publications-across-uk-face-covid-19-cuts/.

McIntyre, K. (2016) What makes "good" news newsworthy? *Communication Research Reports*, 33(3), 223–230.

Moore, M. (2015) Plurality and local media. In: Barnett S. and Townend J. (Eds.), *Media power and plurality* (pp. 65–82). London: Palgrave Macmillan.

Olsen, R.K., Pickard, V., and Westlund, O. (2020) Communal news work: COVID-19 calls for collective funding of journalism. *Digital Journalism*, 8(5), 673–680.

Sherehiy, B., and Karwowski, W. (2014) The relationship between work organization and workforce agility in small manufacturing enterprises. *International Journal of Industrial Ergonomics*, 44(3), 466–473.

Tobitt, C. (2020a) Coronavirus crisis could force closure of 'most' hyperlocal news publishers within weeks. *Press Gazette*, March 27, www.pressgazette.co.uk/coronavirus-crisis-could-force-closure-of-most-hyperlocal-news-publishers-within-weeks/.

Tobitt, C. (2020b) Millions more seek out local news online during pandemic, figures show. *Press Gazette*, August 20, www.pressgazette.co.uk/millions-more-seek-out-local-news-online-during-pandemic-figures-show/.

Tobitt, C. (2020c) Press Gazette survey reveals devastating impact three months of lockdown would have on news media industry. *Press Gazette*, April 20, www.pressgazette.co.uk/press-gazette-survey-reveals-devastating-impact-three-months-of-lockdown-would-have-on-news-media-industry/.

Tobbitt, C., and Majid, A. (2021) ABCs: UK local newspaper sales hard-hit by pandemic with dailies down by average of 18%. *Press Gazette*, February 21, www.pressgazette.co.uk/regional-print-abcs-daily-circulation-down-average-18-per-cent-second-half-2020/.

Van Kerkhoven, M., and Bakker, P. (2014) The hyperlocal in practice: innovation, creativity and diversity. *Digital Journalism*, 2(3), 296–309.

Wahl-Jorgensen, K. (2020) *Evidence submission for the inquiry into the future of journalism House of Lords Communications and Digital Committee.* London: House of Lords Communications and Digital Committee.

Wahl-Jorgensen, K. (2021) Precarity in community journalism start-ups: the deep story of sacrifice. In: Steiner L. and Chadha K. (Eds.), *Precarity in journalism.* London and New York, NY: Routledge.

Wahl-Jorgensen, K. (forthcoming). Community journalism as responsible journalism. In: Lynch J. and Rice C. (Eds.), *Responsible journalism in conflicted societies: trust and public service across new and old divides.* London and New York, NY: Routledge.

Williams, A., Barnett, S., Harte, D., and Townend, J. (2014) The state of UK hyperlocal community news: findings from a survey of practitioners. Working paper, available at: http://orca.cf.ac.uk/68425/1/hyperlocal-community-news-in-the-uk-2014.pdf.

4 Supporting hyperlocal reporting

Global funding, local voices

Sarah Cheverton

Introduction

This chapter examines a community reporting project that took place in 2020 to capture the impact of COVID-19 on local residents in Portsmouth, UK. The project was run by *Star & Crescent*, a not-for-profit, online-only independent community news operation, and was funded by two external philanthropic grant funding sources. The COVID-19 Support Fund was established in spring 2020 by the European Journalism Centre and the Facebook Journalism Project to support innovation projects that would help news organisations or freelancers "engage their communities during the pandemic" (European Journalism Centre 2020). *Star & Crescent* received €5000 from this funding. At a similar time, the Public Interest News Foundation established a COVID-19 Emergency Fund that drew on funds from the UK charity Joseph Rowntree Reform Trust and the US-based non-profit Internews (Public Interest News Foundation 2020). Here the emphasis was on supporting small-scale (turnover below £2 million) news publishers suffering financial hardship as a result of the impact of the pandemic. *Star & Crescent* received £3000 from this fund. In both funds, the criteria prioritised independent community news publishers over legacy media and sought to support public interest news. This case study is both an overview of how such funding is spent by independent media to create value for its audiences, and also a wider reflection on the challenges facing local news publishers in the context of the continuing decline in revenue streams for legacy local news that threatens their ability to undertake public interest local reporting. I draw on my own reflections as editor of *Star & Crescent* and also on interviews with three citizen-journalists who were funded as part of the project. The intention here is to explore the opportunities and challenges represented by the project and the value of the funding to *Star & Crescent* as an organisation.

DOI: 10.4324/9781003173144-5

Context

Local journalism by largely corporately – owned legacy media has historically been funded by newspaper sales and advertising income, both of which have been subject to a slow, but occasionally, rapid decline in recent decades. The decline has had a well-documented impact on local public interest journalism (Franklin 2005; Morrison 2011), something the UK Government's Cairncross Review (Department for Digital, Culture, Media and Sport 2019) drew attention to in noting the importance of ensuring the sustainability of local news in the public interest. It is not just high-impact investigative journalism that matters, the review argued, but also covering everyday matters in local politics and governance (2019: 17). In an attempt to ensure such reporting continues, subsidy has arrived in the form of schemes such as the Local Democracy Reporting Scheme (LDRS), funded by the BBC licence fee, and Facebook's Community News Project, both of which directly pay commercial legacy media for local journalists reporting in the public interest. Alongside this, experiments in online subscriptions, paywalls, and membership schemes have had variable degrees of success. Ultimately, the transfer of advertising revenue from legacy local news publishers to an online advertising market dominated by Google and Facebook (see Evens 2018 for an overview) has yet to be adequately replaced and in many nations (see examples in Sjøvaag and Krumsvik 2018; Hess and Waller 2020), attempts are underway to regulate or rebalance the inequity of advertising revenue between these two sectors.

The decline in mainstream provision has been mirrored by the growth in small independent community news publishers that have emerged across the country, offering highly localised content (also referred to as hyperlocals – see Harte et al. 2018). These are often citizen-led and represent a diversity of journalistic practices, working for the most part directly with local communities. A range of organisational and income-generation models are employed in this nascent independent sector, from small businesses to cooperatives and including the use of subscriptions, crowdfunding, and funding grants. As many have noted, there has been a high reliance on volunteers (Radcliffe 2015; Williams et al. 2014; Cook et al. 2016). While local journalism is increasingly becoming the focus of state support, this has not been equally accessible by independent community news publishers, for whom the funding landscape is often more complex and whose long-term prospect of survival is more precarious (Radcliffe 2015). In recent years, many community news publishers have looked to grant funding to sustain their operations, including philanthropic funding from charities and foundations in the UK and abroad. This funding has enabled many organisations to experiment with participatory, citizen-led approaches to newsgathering and freed them (at least temporarily) from reliance on a volunteer workforce. Some funding sources are supported, often indirectly, by these same "big tech" companies, including both Facebook and Google, and some – though by no means all – have included independent community publishers as recipients. A small number of other funders (e.g. the UK innovation foundation Nesta, the Carnegie UK Trust, the Public Interest News Foundation) have specifically targeted the community news sector, aiming to both financially support and strategically develop it.

Scott Rodgers has referred to these last types of funding programmes as "embody[ing] a new kind of informational philanthropy attempting to strategically curate and build knowledge" (2018: 75) around the development of digital, community news. This is embodied in the growing number of funding programmes targeting hyperlocal community news publishers. In addition to direct funding, there is also the offer of additional support such as mentoring and specialist advice, specifically aimed at developing capacity and sustainability. For example, Rodgers examines a programme called Destination Local (spanning 2013–2017), delivered by Nesta, a former government quango funded by an endowment from the National Lottery that relaunched as a charity in 2012. Destination Local, alongside providing funding to independent community publishers, also "sought to anticipate, assemble and animate a 'space' for UK hyperlocal media production" (ibid.: 76). Rodgers highlights a tension often found in hyperlocal funding programmes as the "sector" extends far beyond the independent publishers who run local news organisations to include "a field space of researchers, policy-makers, entrepreneurs and technologists" (80) and more. This makes such projects not only an "opportunity" for publishers, but also for the funders themselves, and for other associated professionals. Thus, it could be argued, the supporting, researching, and representing of independent community news publishers may currently be a more sustainable industry than the publishing itself. In examining a series of case studies related to Destination Local, Rodgers notes a tension for funding recipients: "[it] was less about successful projects, rather experimentation, and cultivating a hyperlocal 'space'" (2017: 9). Harte highlights that such funding sources may even exacerbate rather than relieve the "precarious existence" (2016: 45) of some hyperlocals in his case study of the *Tyburn Mail* in Castle Vale, Birmingham. He notes its shifting form from a not-for-profit, to a limited company, to a charity, in its struggle to continue operations and meet funders' expectations. Most funding grants are not aimed at supporting the core operations of local news publishers, leaving them facing the same fundamental challenge as the legacy media – who or what pays for local news – arguably with less support from the state and global technology companies, and less well-established lobbying power.

The COVID-19 Community Reporting Project, Portsmouth

Star & Crescent was originally founded in February 2015 by myself and Tom Sykes, working as volunteers with a small group of local writers. We began by publishing as a bimonthly online magazine, comprising around 40 articles per edition, before moving to a more regular publishing model of about three to five articles a week by 2017. We were working with a broad base of local residents, community groups, and organisations, which led us to set up a not-for-profit company, Star & Crescent Community Media CIC, to provide a legal framework for our operations that would also allow us to become eligible for funding programmes open to social enterprises. *Star & Crescent* works with local residents in a variety of ways: accepting submissions of opinion pieces, reviews, and human-interest features from residents; as volunteers supporting the website or organisation; and by training local residents as community reporters who are then able to pursue news stories and reports. *Star & Crescent* does not have a "real-world" office, and instead (prior to the pandemic) worked both virtually with contributors, and in "real-world" community spaces (e.g. libraries, community centres) working face to face, for example, to deliver training programmes and undertake interviews. Aiming to complement, not to compete, with Portsmouth's long-established newspaper, *The News* (owned by JPI Media), *Star & Crescent* prioritises working directly with local residents, communities, and organisations to bring missing or under-represented perspectives, voices, and stories to the mainstream.

The project arose at a time when *Star & Crescent* had been greatly affected by the pandemic. As a predominantly volunteer-run operation, *Star & Crescent* was not hit by a loss of income as a result of COVID-19, but by the loss of one of our two full-time volunteers. Both volunteers were working with the publication to gain professional experience in local news reporting, social media, and publishing and were responsible for running the website on a daily basis. Without them, *Star & Crescent*'s operations would grind to a sudden, immediate halt. This was the first time *Star & Crescent* received funding to deliver our core operation, that is, working with local residents to tell stories that are missing from the local news landscape. However, it had received previous small grants: in 2015, funding from Nesta supported participation in an action research project; and in 2017 grant funding supported the changing of the publication's legal status to a Community Interest Company and development of the website. Further, in 2018, a partnership with the Centre for Investigative Journalism (funded by the Joseph Rowntree Charitable Trust) was used to train local residents as community reporters. The grant funding from the European Journalism Centre and the Public Interest News Foundation differed from other support in that it directly funded reporting, work that is normally delivered by the team working as volunteers, often in partnership with local residents, communities, or organisations. The broader backdrop of COVID-19 deepened the crisis already being experienced by many news publishers and seemed to act as a catalyst for some funders to support the delivery of local news directly, as opposed to supporting projects based on innovation, for example. The funding thus allowed *Star & Crescent* to continue operating, at least for the duration of the funding.

As editor, I applied for both the European Journalism Centre and Public Interest News Foundation funds to report on the impact of COVID-19 on individuals from groups being disproportionately affected by the pandemic, namely: female entrepreneurs and small business owners; people of colour communities; migrant communities; refugees and asylum seekers; people with disabilities or long-term health conditions (with a focus on shielding from COVID-19); and voluntary sector organisations. Alongside our remaining full-time volunteer, I recruited three more local residents as paid freelancers to create a team of four COVID-19 community reporters. Two of the new recruits had worked with *Star & Crescent* as volunteers in the past and one, who was a local leader in the small business community, had previous writing experience. Our main criterion was for each reporter to have a relationship to the area they were reporting on and a strong active local network they could draw on for their reporting. For example, the reporter on people with disabilities lives with a disability and was shielding from the pandemic. As a community activist, they had a broad network of local contacts related to disability and long-term health issues that they could draw on for their interviews. The community reporters approached interviewees from their own networks to be interviewed on the impact of COVID-19 on them as individuals, community groups, or organisations. In addition, each reporter wrote an article introducing themselves as a COVID-19 Community Reporter and inviting people to get in touch with them directly (although this did not yield many results, and did not lead to any of the final interviews). Some organisations, including a local domestic violence charity and a local charity supporting refugees, had worked with *Star & Crescent* before, and relevant contacts were made available to the reporters to decide whether to approach them for interview. The interviews were conducted using video-conferencing platforms, recorded, and then transcribed by a small team of volunteers, before being returned to the reporter. Each reporter then produced a draft article from the transcript: either an edited (for clarity and length) version of the full interview or, in the case of a small number of interviewees, a report of the interview, including quotes taken directly from the interview. These edited reports were passed back to the interviewee, who then liaised with the reporter to ensure edits accurately represented their words. Reporters were encouraged to prioritise the voice of the interviewee "in their own words" in these drafts, which were then passed to me as an editor for final approval, before being published on the website.

There were several aims here: to increase the diversity of our workforce, given the under-representation of minorities and marginalised groups in the wider news media landscape; to build trust with community members and organisations working with under-represented and marginalised groups; and to prioritise reporting direct experiences in detail in the words of interviewees over traditional "objective" reporting on these groups from the "outside." In meeting these aims, we hoped to increase representation and understanding of the diverse lived experiences of different groups in the local community.

The experiences of the COVID-19 community reporters

The outputs of the project were one-to-one, in-depth interviews either reflecting individual experiences of the pandemic or local business and voluntary sector leaders talking about the impact of COVID-19 on their organisations. Across the project, the community reporters conducted 36 interviews, resulting in 60 articles. The articles were published between August and November 2020. The approach to writing up the interviews was to prioritise the words of participants. Indeed, most interviews were versions of the original interview transcript, edited for clarity and length. Many interviews were published in several parts, across several days of the week, allowing interviewees to see the edited interview upon publication and work with the reporter to clarify anything they felt was unclear. This iterative approach was deliberate and reflected our aim to be participatory and citizen-led.

Through semi-structured interviews I conducted with three of the community reporters (the fourth reporter was not available), I identified three central shared themes from their reflections on the project: the impact of telling stories in a different way and prioritising marginalised voices; personal and professional impacts on the reporters themselves; and the impacts of grant funding on the project and reporters.

Storytelling in a different way and prioritising marginalised voices

All reporters talked about the value and social benefits of prioritising marginalised voices in the project. Some related this to a lack or an absence of such reporting in the mainstream media:

> I was able to interview two refugees/asylum seekers in Britain in a non-biased way because obviously the way it's reported in the mainstream isn't what it is, isn't the reality for a lot of those people.
>
> (Participant 1)

> I can't identify a lot with the people in the news because on the whole, they're powerful people making decisions about our lives […] but during the pandemic, all of a sudden, the media was interested in how people's lives were being affected by the pandemic.
>
> (Participant 2)

> [Among] all the sensationalism and all of the propaganda that was going, it was very rare you found real stories from real people who are dealing with [Covid-19] in the thick of things […] especially in a time that's about clickbait and sensationalism and trying to get as much traffic as possible.
>
> (Participant 3)

The reporters felt the project built a lot of trust in the local community for *Star & Crescent* as an organisation and raised our profile, particularly within the communities, we focused on for the project:

> I think we've built up more trust. I think what the project's really done has brought us to the forefront to the local community [because] we are prepared to report in depth on social issues and at the same time we do that ethically.
>
> (Participant 1)

Part of the reason for this was related to the perceived social impact of the project on the wider community:

> I think [the project] can open the ears of many people who weren't listening before [...] I hope it awakens people to [think]: 'what can I do to help other people, how can I connect to them when they're different from me? [...] Because I think the media that we have [can mean] people can be so desensitised.
>
> (Participant 3)

One reporter noted the impact of the project on interviewees:

> I found there was an eagerness and a want amongst people who'd been shielding to tell people about their experiences and to say what was working for them and what wasn't [...] if a space has been opened up for people's experiences, opinions and insights to be listened to then that's a very good and positive impact.
>
> (Participant 2)

Another highlighted that the project enabled richer conversations with interviewees:

> [The project] gave us the leverage to really talk to [interviewees] and get down to the nitty gritty of everything, especially with the intersectionality of what so many people are going through, so you have racism, you have Black Lives Matter, you have Covid-19 [...]
>
> (Participant 3)

These conversations often led us to issues that surprised reporters and led them into areas that are less commonly represented in the mainstream media, for example: "Faith played a big role in some of the people I interviewed [and] that's not a perspective you're seeing a lot in many articles on Covid-19" (participant 3).

Personal and professional impact

All the reporters talked about a personal impact of feeling nervous before the project started, which was related to the funding and an awareness that being paid shifted them from volunteers to "professionals": "I was absolutely terrified because it was a national project and an international project. It was my first major project at all, freelancing" (participant 1). The development of professional skills was highlighted as a positive impact for the reporters, for example in developing a new career path:

It's my first major freelance project and I've got the experience and the back[ground] knowledge of this so I can do this, basically. And I wouldn't have been able to do that had I not done the year and a half worth of volunteering for *Star & Crescent*.

(Participant 1)

Another reporter highlighted how working on the project had (somewhat reluctantly) improved her technological skills: "I hate working digitally [...] it gave me a good, good opportunity to get better at it" (participant 2). For one reporter, the project reinforced their belief in the professional ethos they brought to their "normal" day job: "It confirmed a lot of things [...] especially when it comes to collaboration and partnership, [it] definitely impacts my work in pushing that even further" (participant 3). All three reporters felt the project had built up their confidence.

Another personal impact came as a direct result of the isolation of the pandemic and the opportunity the project gave reporters to connect with others:

I felt like the opportunity to talk to people about shielding would give me a better insight into other people's lives, as I say, at a time when I was deprived of that social contact.

(Participant 2)

[A rewarding element was] being able to talk to people about their experience and how so many different things intersected.

(Participant 3)

Finally, in addition to creating employment for local residents, there was another, indirect, social impact of the project, as one of our reporters donated half of her freelance fee to her daughter's school:

I gave half of it to [my daughter's] school because they worked so hard during the pandemic [...] I don't agree at all with the Victorian concept of wealthy philanthropists, but I agree even less with deliberately underfunding public services, so for me that was another, you can put that in the category of the impacts that the project had.

(Participant 2)

The perceived impact of the project being grant funded

One of the main constraints presented by the project was time. Externally funded projects are often required to be completed in a timeframe set by the funder, and our bid had been ambitious in its goals to be competitive and secure the funds. The reporters felt this constraint most keenly, with all referring to the pressure of time: "I thought, oh goodness me, eight interviews [in] eight weeks [...] that seemed like quite a challenge" (participant 2). The time constraints were felt particularly by the two reporters working across both strands of the funding, as they effectively had two competing deadlines: "I went in at the deep end, I decided to do two major projects at the same time" (participant 1). As a result, we extended the reporting deadline on both strands of work as far as we could, adjusted workloads accordingly, and stepped in as a team to support each other with particularly demanding workloads as deadlines approached.

Two reporters described a fear of "letting down" *Star & Crescent* and the other reporters if something went wrong with the project, which one linked to the fact that it was being "paid for": "this was a big project that I was getting paid for [...] you cannot let *Star & Crescent* down on this" (participant 1). One reporter who had professional experience of working on grant-funded projects in the voluntary sector felt a sense of pressure, knowing that *Star & Crescent* would be expected to "deliver" outcomes to demonstrate the value of receiving such funding:

> I think with any project, all you can do is take one day, one step, at a time [...] It's easier said than done sometimes, especially when there's so much pressure and you're applying for funding and you have to report back, so it's understandable that, and those funding bodies have expectations as well.
>
> (Participant 3)

Reflections on the value of project funding

Ultimately, the challenges facing *Star & Crescent* as a small not-for-profit community publisher (including capacity building, funding investigative journalism, business planning etc.) are unlikely to be addressed by short-term grant funding alone. By early 2021, after the projects ended, the website had to pause operations to look for funding again. However, during its lifetime, the project enabled *Star & Crescent* to employ our former full-time volunteer as a freelancer, to employ a local female business leader, and to employ two local residents who have worked with us over the last five years as volunteers, one of whom was a community reporter we had trained as part of the Centre for Investigative Journalism partnership project. Providing a route from volunteering to paid employment in community news is an important part of *Star & Crescent*'s organisational ethos and part of how the organisation contributes, albeit modestly, to the local community and economy. Our aim is to support residents interested in working in local media, particularly those who face barriers to entering the profession, for example, people from working-class backgrounds, ethnic minorities, women, and those living with a disability or long-term health condition.

Although the project allowed us to focus on our core operations, it also generated additional, unforeseen, and unpaid workloads that came as a result of working exclusively digitally. In particular, the daily management of the project was a far heavier workload than we had anticipated when costing the projects. This workload ended up being mostly unpaid and time-consuming. To prioritise the core reporting, we focused the majority of the funding on the freelance community reporters and relied on a volunteer workforce for editing, transcribing interviews, and finance management. This would not be viable moving forward as these workloads would become more significant and would require payment to avoid exploitation of volunteers.

Conclusion: supporting local news in the public interest

The experience of the project raised a lot of issues for *Star & Crescent* as an organisation but also highlights some of the challenges and opportunities facing the independent local news sector across the UK. Funding that is targeted partially or exclusively towards independent community news publishers is scarcer and smaller than the subsidies aimed at legacy news media and rarely supports the core operations of small publishers (largely being focused on "innovation" projects or organisational development; the funds from the Public Interest News Foundation were a rare exception in this). If the state, private business, and/or philanthropic funding bodies want to address the "local news crisis," then a broader awareness of the crisis may be vital. For many independent community news publishers, the crisis is far less about the collapse of advertising and sales revenues in corporately owned local newspapers than about how to move away from a reliance on volunteerism. Indeed, the crisis can be viewed as two-fold: the collapse of a business and revenue model; and the long-term decline of local reporting in the public interest. Further, it is important to trace this dual crisis in the wider context of the history of local news publishing in the UK (see Matthews 2017a, b) as a number of independent news publishers came into creation as a result of this decline in local reporting and are actively working to identify a sustainable future for it, in a variety of ways. As a result, the mission, operations, and business models of many independent local news publishers frequently differ significantly from those of legacy news publishers and "one-size-fits-all" solutions, or those designed exclusively by funders and legacy media without independent publishers in the room, frequently miss both the needs of independent publishers and misunderstand the value of their participatory approaches.

For many not-for-profits like *Star & Crescent*, one solution may well be a mixed economy, including consultancy and trading, membership schemes, events, and donations, alongside grant funding. For organisations such as these, there is an urgent need for capacity building across the sector that supports independent community news publishers to identify, develop, and share best practice in these areas, enabling them to become sustainable and preserve their independence. How funding bodies want to support this work in the future will depend on their awareness of the whole local news landscape, in particular, its complexity, diversity, and history. If funders do not have this awareness, they run the risk of propping up the failing business model of legacy local news, while the innovation taking place in the independent sector goes unsupported, becomes far more precarious, and, in the long-term, perhaps less viable.

References

Cook, C., Geels, K. & Bakker, P. (2016) *Hyperlocal revenues in the UK and Europe. Mapping the road to sustainability and resilience.* London: Nesta. Available at: https://media.nesta.org.uk/documents/hyperlocal-revenues-in-the-uk-and-europe-report.pdf (Accessed 13 March 2021).

Department for Digital, Culture, Media and Sport. (2019) *Cairncross review: a sustainable future for journalism.* London: Department for Digital, Culture, Media and Sport. Available at: www.gov.uk/government/publications/the-cairncross-review-a-sustainable-future-for-journalism (Accessed 13 March 2021).

European Journalism Centre. (2020) *38 News organisations and freelancers receive grant funding as part of the Engagement and Innovation Funds.* Available at: https://europeanjournalism.fund/news/engagement-innovation-fund-recipients-wave1 (Accessed 25 March 2021).

Evens, T. (2018) Media economics and transformation in a digital Europe. In: d'Haenens, L., Sousa, H. & Trappel, J. (Eds.), *Comparative media policy, regulation and governance in Europe. Unpacking the policy cycle* (pp. 41–54). Bristol: Intellect.

Franklin, B. (2005) McJournalism: the local press and the McDonaldization thesis. In: Stuart, A. (Ed.), *Journalism: critical issues* (pp. 137–150). Maidenhead: Open University Press.

Harte, D. (2016) "Tell it like it is": the role of community not-for-profit media in regeneration and reputational change. *Ethical Space: The International Journal of Communication Ethics*, 13(2): 35–47.

Harte, D., Howells, R. & Williams, A. (2018) *Hyperlocal journalism: the decline of local newspapers and the rise of online community news*. London: Routledge.

Hess, K. & Waller, L.J. (2020) Local newspapers and coronavirus: conceptualising connections, comparisons and cures. *Media International Australia*, 178(1): 21–35.

Matthews, R. (2017a). *The history of the Provincial Press in England*. London: Bloomsbury.

Matthews, R. (2017b) The socio-local newspaper: creating a sustainable future for the legacy provincial news industry. In: Berglez, P., Olausson, U. & Ots, M. (Eds.), *What is sustainable journalism?: integrating the environmental, social, and economic challenges of journalism* (pp. 333–350). Oxford: Peter Lang.

Morrison, J. (2011) Spin, smoke-filled rooms and the decline of council reporting by British local newspapers: the slow demise of town hall transparency. In: Charles, A. & Stewart, G. (Eds.), *The end of journalism: news in the twenty first century* (pp. 193–209). Bern: Peter Lang.

Public Interest News Foundation. (2020) *Supporting independent news publishers during the Covid-19 crisis*. Available at: www.publicinterestnews.org.uk/emergency-fund (Accessed 25 March 2021).

Radcliffe, D. (2015) *Where are we now? UK hyperlocal media and community journalism in 2015*. Nesta & Centre for Community Journalism, University of Cardiff. Available at: https://ourlocality.org/hyperlocally/files/2015/11/here_and_now_uk_hyperlocal_media_today.pdf (Accessed 13 March 2021).

Rodgers, S. (2017) Roots and fields: excursions through place, space and local in hyperlocal media. *Media, Culture & Society*, 40(6): 856–874.

Rodgers, S. (2018) Digitizing localism: anticipating, assembling and animating a 'space' for UK hyperlocal media production. *International Journal of Cultural Studies*, 21(1): 73–89.

Sjøvaag, H. & Krumsvik, A.H. (2018) In search of journalism funding. *Journalism Practice*, 12(9): 1201–1219.

Williams, A., Barnett, S., Harte, D. & Townend, J. (2014) *The state of hyperlocal community news in the UK: findings from a survey of practitioners*. Available at: https://hyperlocalsurvey.files.wordpress.com/2014/07/hyperlocal-community-news-in-the-uk-2014.pdf (Accessed 13 March 2021).

5 Who's cashing in? Reappraising the economic value of independent community news

Clare Cook and Coral Milburn-Curtis

Introduction

The republication of stories between different media organisations in the UK news supply chain is commonplace. However, the practices of linking, copying, or story follow-up are not standardised. From the days when newspapers each tracked clippings from other titles, many journalists rework stories under fair dealing, particularly for the purposes of reporting current events, reviews, or quotations (Copyright, Designs and Patent Act 1988). National news organisations have long relied on the local press to pump-prime their reporting. Regional newspapers trawl competitor news sites for ideas and independent and community news sites review national and regional news agendas to see if stories can be repositioned with local contacts or story angles. A free flow of news items is part of "open" news sourcing practices where content "produsers" serve as gatewatchers monitoring the content of other publications (Bruns 2014: 185).

Divergent practices for story republication and attribution have been drawn into focus, potentially illuminating the boundaries of what constitutes fair dealing for those wanting to justify reusing copy from smaller outlets, agencies, and freelancers. In 2017, the *Independent* declined to pay a freelance court reporter for details of a story they lifted from Wales Online, claiming "there is no copyright in news" (Ponsford 2017). Wales Online did pay for the original story. In a separate case, Rochdale Online was awarded £200 plus costs of £170 from the *Manchester Evening News* at a small claims court after it sustained an investigation into the expenses of their member of parliament, Simon Danczuk, based on a Freedom of Information request (Ponsford 2017a). A week after publication, the *Manchester Evening News* used the article without permission, without credit for Rochdale Online neither through affordances of link-based distribution, and without

DOI: 10.4324/9781003173144-6

payment, claiming it had not copied verbatim; therefore, there was no breach of copyright. The piece was syndicated by Rochdale Online to *The Sun* and *The Guardian*. This "sweat of the brow" verdict not only validated the need for more robust adherence to copyright laws but also for a fundamental review of the economic value of content production. These cases point to the important question of how the ongoing future contribution of independent and community news rests on a systematic rebalance if a diverse landscape of public interest publishers is to preserve their ability to successfully monetise their content to fund already endangered grassroots newsgathering.

Such imperatives are heightened because of the lack of financial security of independent news operations (Ofcom 2009) with far-reaching implications for the medium-to-long term resilience of publications existing in the long tail of journalism. Much scholarly work has focussed on hyperlocal media, a term typically used to explain grassroots online news or content services pertaining to a town or small geographically defined "local" community (Radcliffe 2012). While research from an economic perspective is limited, mapping work has found most earned relatively small sums, with 23 from a sample of 62 making less than £100 a month (Williams et al. 2014). A pan-European study, including 13 sites from the UK (Cook et al. 2016), found the most effective revenue for sustainability to be display advertising, with some lucrative income from native formats. Notably, there was a resurgence in print products based on the affordance of discoverability, which impacts advertising revenues. By way of an indicative size by turnover, most Western hyperlocals made less than €35,000. Few hyperlocals have the time and resources to focus on earning revenues, attracting investments, or making sites attractive to advertisers (Schaffer 2007). A range of toolkits and guides have been created by the Knight Foundation (McLella and Patel 2011) and Nesta's Destination Local programme (Radcliffe 2012, 2015) and by Carnegie Trust (Pennycook 2015; Tenor 2017) to boost business practice. A persistent precarity in operations arises as many spend more on content production and sustaining operations than they should, resulting in self-exploitation (Harte et al. 2019).

Given the overall dominance of a shoestring model, tensions exist between independents and corporate regional and national media over the republication of stories, and the revenues this generates. There is little known about how to get effective remuneration from mainstream to independent and local publishers for the content they provide, nor how to broker fairer payments for news republication between publishers. While we know many operations have diversified revenues, with the most typical revenue model being made up of three primary income streams (Cook and Bakker 2019), syndication revenues specifically are a blind spot in both scholarly and practice-based studies. Certainly, syndicated opportunities – to make content available to other publishers via remunerated permissions – are sporadic. What scant data exist for European independents says little of the lived experience of generating income from such media-to-media content sales (Cook et al. 2016). Therefore, advancing the understanding of the economic payback of content production for media of all shapes and sizes in the supply chain sheds new light on a possible revenue stream. It is a timely inquiry as mainstream news providers are increasingly demanding a level playing field for smaller competitors against technology giants and a fair market for consumers (Hern 2020), while at the same time larger publishing groups are cutting back on jobs and needing alternative ways to produce high volumes of content.

To fill this gap, this chapter draws on exploratory work conducted in spring 2020 during the alpha development phase of a project to build a platform called Ping! (Omni Digital 2020). The platform works by pooling content from members of the Independent Community News Network (ICNN) in one content management system from its national network of more than a hundred media organisations. The platform's goal is to generate new revenues from syndication sales of tiered, pooled community news feeds or one-off content sales to other news media in the UK, innovating and diversifying the UK news supply chain by quickly connecting the content of grassroots journalists with larger publishers. The beta trial in early 2021 focussed on providing immediate access of corporate regional publishers to the pooled ICNN news production.

The approach fits with other initiatives innovating from the supply chain side, such as sales of integrated court data to the media, legal, and financial sectors via digital search and tracking service Courtsdesk or international story sales from the global south to the global north with platforms such as MediaBridge, Paydesk, and StoryMarket. Elsewhere, schemes such as the Local Democracy Reporting Service formalise a framework for credited content sharing in the supply chain. Stories written by democracy reporters are shared with more than 900 media titles and outlets in the UK as part of the Local News Partnerships scheme. Independents benefit from the content and through shared credit with other reporters where content is copied, edited, or incorporated into new pieces of work. It was hoped hyperlocal publishers would see a larger slice of the scheme, but the majority of the human resource benefits went to large newspaper groups as the majority lacked the scale to deliver on the contracts. Only a handful of the 60 contracts were assigned to independent and hyperlocal publishers (BBC 2017).

The chapter asks what incomes are currently being generated from syndication by ICNN members as part of their revenue model. It assesses attitudes and practices around current republication and story linking from independent and mainstream news perspectives. In so doing, it sheds light on the value of public interest journalism in the UK supply chain of news.

Methodology

The data are made up of three phases focused around the creation of Ping!. The first phase was an online benchmarking survey circulated to members of the ICNN. As sites have matured and diversified, there has been a move towards a broader appreciation of independent and community media, rather than the more restrictive term hyperlocals. The ICNN has eligibility and quality controls across a national network and so offered potential "sellers." A survey of 55 questions available in early 2019 had 33 respondents from across the UK (see Figure 5.1). It was created primarily to inform the development of the Ping! platform and to strengthen our understanding of syndication as lived practice in the UK news supply chain. The second phase used a purposive sampling strategy, as we sought to engage participants with the two-month alpha trial of the Ping! platform, to fine-tune the development of the platform from a technological and usability perspective, as well as improve our understanding of content sales between independents and larger news outlets. Ten participant interviews were conducted from

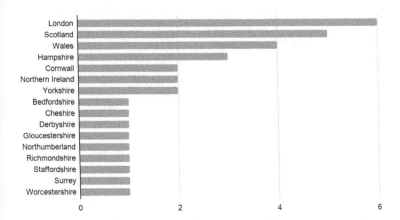

Figure 5.1 Distribution of interview respondents by geographic range.

ICNN members in January 2020 covering 40 questions. To address potential limitations of this strategy, care was taken not to generalise to a larger population. Both phases captured core data, including revenues, positioning, story production rates, and experiences with copy reproduction, linkage, and content sales. Data from the benchmark and alpha surveys were merged into one database ($n = 35$) once respondent overlaps were removed.

In phase three, ten semi-structured interviews were conducted in May 2020 to capture perspectives from editors, senior reporters, or managers as potential content "buyers." Interviewees were selected to represent a range of media ownership structures and in geographic scope, recognised typically as mainstream news. Regional, national, and international public service news titles across broadcast, print, and online formats were included as were freelancers, specialist investigative services, and press wires. The sample included the BBC, Archant, Reach PLC, Reuters, Guardian, Daily Mail, ITV, and the Bureau of Investigative Journalism to best illustrate a wide variety of commissioning and story republication practices. We also wanted to learn about journalists' interest in using independent and community content; when and how this would be possible, and the basis on which they would do that. Purposive sampling allowed us to approach news organisations in the media ecosystem working in similar geographic areas to the alpha trial publishers. Each interview lasted 30 minutes and included five parts: story sourcing routines, interest in hyperlocal content, trending practices, syndication arrangements, and story commissioning budgets. Quantitative results were sorted into nominal categorical data such as total revenues and audience figures. Medians were calculated in preference to the mean where there was a risk of abnormal skew. The qualitative data from all three phases were transcribed and thematically coded.

Revenues for independent and community media

The combined quantitative core data from phases one and two confirmed findings from previous work that the independent and community news sector is highly heterogeneous. The spread of core data was such that it was difficult to present a typical independent or community media (see Table 5.1). The largest site in terms of monthly website unique users was 225,000 and the smallest 1,000. However, these are still notably smaller than digital readership rates at corporate regionals, Reach PLC being the first UK news publisher to cross 40 million unique visitors in a single month (Tobitt 2019). Legal structures ranged from community interest

Table 5.1 Core data of independent and community media by medians

	Median
Website users per month	20,000
Area covered in square miles	40
Year established	2011
Output number of stories per day	4

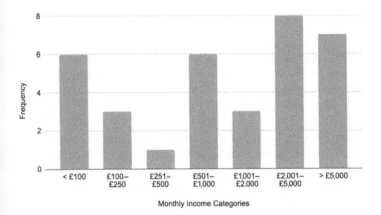

Figure 5.2 Monthly earnings by nominal category ($n = 35$).

company, limited liability company, sole trader, and company limited by guarantee. Sites ranged from launch in 1998 to 2018.

Overall the indicators advanced knowledge on financial results (Cook et al. 2016; Harte et al. 2019) but show earnings that are still modest. In the reporting period between April 2017 and 2018, the best-performing sites earned £180,000 while six made no money (see Figure 5.2). The median annual earnings were £14,603. The primary revenue stream was display advertising, online or in print. There were notable successes in sponsored sections and articles. Only four sites earned revenues from programmatic advertising and several reported reliance on the Google tool AdSense. To earn more money from classified, there was interest in providing local business offers, as direct advertising sales generated from real-world business clients paid better than programmatic. Others said a dedicated sales' person working on commission helped boost income. Overall, local advertising sales were the most profitable income stream but "it's a very tough climate," according to one ICNN respondent.

Table 5.2 Income stream rates comparing story sales, print adverts, and digital subscribers

	Median in £	Range
Total estimated earnings from sale of stories to other media (*n* = 5)	380	50–600
Price for one sold story (*n* = 5)	80	50–150
Price for fixed-term full page print advert (*n* = 6)	362.50	198–600
Monthly revenue from digital members/subscribers (*n* = 5)	50	35–660

Sustainable revenues varied (see Table 5.2). Print advertising remained the best return on investment in terms of rate per unit. Six media with print products charged a median price for a full page, fixed-term advert of £362.50. Data showed fledgling transition to audience revenues with only five sites reporting any income from digital membership or subscriptions. This included tentative steps to nuanced messaging for donations to support the public interest cause. Success was attributed to slow, organic, but real, growth based on the perceived value of editorial independence both online and in print. Increased traffic to the website was linked to increased revenues.

Economic opportunities for syndication

The data detailed revenues generated from syndication by UK independent news sites to other media. Independent news media that have staff with backgrounds as freelancers were better placed to sell content. There was little consistency in remuneration rates and the commission process across diverse mainstream media varied in efficiency. In our data, seven news outlets attempted to sell content and five earned money from selling stories with the median rate being £80 for a story (Table 5.2). When asked if any official syndication agreements were in place only three had arrangements: with Cascade Media, NLA Media Access, Wales News Service, and an informal agreement between two hyperlocals to share content. All but one alpha respondent said they wanted to generate money from content sales. Most marked content on their sites as copyrighted, in some form. Respondents noted shrinking national media budgets to pay for external content and "the hassle of getting paid" often outweighed production time. Where sales occur, they were haphazard. Overall, resource constraints limit attempts to sell content. To boost story sales, respondents said a syndication service or level of coordination, advice, and training, an automated process and better contacts were needed.

There was a feeling that content was "being stolen" by other media. One ICNN respondent received £50 for a news piece and said: "We might have slogged our guts out and it wouldn't even cover costs, which is disheartening." Another said payments were received but it was rare, and more often for photographs where copyright laws are more clearly defined. More than half ($n = 22$) said their content was not linked to by other publishers or they were not sure. When asked what percentage of content was reproduced by other publishers without payment, four said more than 75% was reproduced. One said, "We often find our stories slightly rewritten, or alluded to, without acknowledgement." Nationals cited as having used content included the Metro, the BBC, online sites such as Mail Online, regional titles such as *Stone and Eccleshall Gazette* and *Yorkshire Evening Post*. Others were student papers such as East London Lines and city title *Evening Standard*. Overall there was no systematic data around content linking and content used by other media. One ICNN member said, "Old-fashioned attitudes about lifting stories are still common."

Supply chain values

Interviews with middle managers and reporters from mainstream media found news organisations indicated high demand for contextual community case studies to improve news narratives through genuine representation of real voices and the inclusion of what matters to people. Such perspectives were noted for their ability to make policy understandable and to humanise complex issues. Journalists were aware of a pressing need to improve relevance for "non-metropolitan Britain" and a desire to "deep listen" and represent communities. In particular, there was an "obsession" for beyond-London representation in the news agenda with independent and community media recognised for the important role they can play for shrinking and time-strapped regional and national teams. National journalists felt uncomfortable as they were disconnected from grassroots and there was recognised value in a network of community reporters deeply connected and in physical proximity with their communities. Reporters wanted to avoid a "fly in, fly out mentality" as it rarely demonstrated story complexity and the nuances of those with lived experiences on the ground. One respondent noted the broader sociopolitical motivation for rich news supply chains: "There is a disconnect with everyone else in the country and it is really dangerous for society."

Mainstream news had in many ways become dependent on grassroots production as an essential part of news sourcing practices. Daily routines included reviewing local, community or independent news websites, and other newspapers for story ideas, which were then advanced by sourcing other quotes and editorial angles. One said, "The best stories get kicked up from local to regional to national." National journalists, it was found, were "terrified that local journalists will pop because we don't have time to phone all the fire services – we rely on them to do that and for that to trickle up." Gaps in content production were part of a broader news supply challenge being plugged by external news providers: sport, international, entertainment, and court copy were often provided by press wires, delivered particularly through email and newsletters. Press Association was cited as one of the leading wire services with deals for varied content bundles. Facebook groups were regularly used as story sources. However, wires and social were rarely deemed to be sources of original content. The increased visibility and digitisation of police and local councils also acting as "news" organisations was blamed for increasing competition for exclusivity. All told, fast-paced news cycles were blamed for driving pressure on reporters to use content they find elsewhere.

Internal syndication within newsroom groups was evolving and was described by one manager as "shared news gathering machines." Syndication of evergreen content and features was conducted internally as a way to fill space in individual titles, maximising opportunities from economies of scale and scope. In our sample, there was no recharge for internal republication of stories and rarely any internal limit on how much a story was used within a newsgroup, although agency content did not always cover regional use. Other regionals were a source of story ideas from the same group to do similar story versions. Regional and nationals shared stories by linking and crediting with by-lines. The BBC had very specific responsibilities for trusted content and standards that were subject to a level of specific regulation and scrutiny.

Linking, copying, or following up stories from other media was not standardised as there were different normative practices of what was acceptable. National journalists noted it was commonplace to "nick regionals and piggyback on the footage." Some outlets used a story and maintained a policy to credit any independent media outlet with either a by-line or by linking to the original article. This was noted to be particularly prevalent when operating under time constraints. Others classed fair dealing as using the idea for the story but seeking original multimedia, attributing only the quotes, or developing a follow-up or new story version. Some publishers made small changes to text, or additions. Others reposted unchanged, without always crediting any original reporting.

In remuneration terms, payments were made for reproducing photographs, but rarely text. There was limited-to-no budget to pay for content produced by other media. One national media manager said: "It is a shrinking business and those rates haven't gone up for 20 years." Remuneration rates were negotiable for exclusive stories, typically at the discretion of a commissioning editor. From our data, standard rates varied from a page lead average of £250–£300 to paying a freelancer for a full day at £250, carrying out a door knock or specific job on behalf of another media at £150 or a story tip off at £80. Specific story rates were negotiable. It was noted to be a competitive space: regional news titles had dedicated staff selling on to nationals and there were many regional news wires.

Mechanisms for economic redress

The supply chain of news remains opaque and a broader mapping study of syndication practices would be useful to practitioners. On a practical level, it takes time and specialised knowledge to build up an individual contact's details at different newsrooms and agencies, across Cavendish Press, Mercury Press and Media, SWNS, Newspaper Monitoring Agency, Ferrari Press Agency, Solent News, to name but a few. Knowledge that expands transparency on the rates paid for wire services or consistent rates for one-off story sales would be a worthy addition. A number of initiatives are ripe for exploration such as understanding how stories are commissioned and used around group syndication systems, including In Your Area by Reach PLC or Project Syndicate from *The Guardian*, alongside new local journalism partnerships between Nextdoor and Bloom Labs.

For syndication to work in practice as a viable revenue stream, our data showed corporate regionals need effectively filtered and robust story selection to avoid flooding them with more information. Bespoke story pitches sensitive to specific news agendas were preferable. Timeliness was an important dimension as stories needed to be offered ahead of the day's news setting. Any offering of a story for sale needed to meet minimum requirements as a complete news package, including multi-media and relevant quotes from multiple perspectives. However, there was also demand from regionals to acquire new multimedia to complement existing stories that could be remunerated. Barriers to overcome included access to willing contacts in the mainstream news, which themselves were places of rapid change.

There is a long way to go to understand how content is valued. There are a number of opportunities to create new value flow: through exclusive private sales, commission fees with independent media, and syndication. Unlike franchise models, syndication approaches provide opportunities to preserve independence while offering some affordances of economies of scale. We need more granularity of how to appropriately charge for and reflect the economic value of content through the broader news supply chain. We have scant scientific analysis of what stories are of use to other media, or when, where, and why. Analysis is ongoing in the Ping! project to review story value based on metastructure and metadata such as quotes, story ideas, originality, and research. Data in the platform can be analysed in two ways: through token allocation against content taxonomies by editorial staff at mainstream news organisations, and qualitative feedback within the system. This will offer indicative results as to which story themes (politics, education, etc.) are of most interest to mainstream publishers and which postcodes. Such a methodology could offer insights into value variance: why some stories from certain geographic areas or content themes are of more value than others.

Syndication offers an opportunity to legitimise access to a diverse range of contacts and stories that are in demand by regional and national media. It can redress the production value of community proximity to meet the need for non-London representation by providing stories and case studies from local and hyperlocal areas. Opening up stories from across independents for use and repurposing is a way of levelling the playing field to boost content production, as regional groups are moving quickly to develop centralised hubs or shared content units. These approaches open an array of new questions relating to the benefits of enabling independents to work together in new ways. Issues of payment and how to distribute the revenues equitably between independent community publishers persist. Alongside, there is need for clarity on codes of practice for the digital connected landscapes and to inform legislative changes on copyright, competition, and fair dealing.

Conclusions

Independent community media are certainly an essential – and currently undervalued – part of the UK news supply chain. More formalised revenue exchanges have the potential to redress, at least in principle, an inequitable use of content by mainstream media of varying size and reach. The exploratory work conducted here demonstrated that there was much potential in creating a network of independent "stringers" or community correspondents as a new way of resourcing journalism that speed up and systemise story flow. There was a shared recognition from both sides that local knowledge and proximity to communities was the value added by independent and community news in the supply chain. Regional newsrooms want to see what is bubbling up in different communities and, faced with downward pressures on staff resourcing and upward pressures on speed and volume, need better ways to find stories. They are also largely open to the idea of partnering with independents via story linking. Editors often work with topics or story angles in mind and want contextual cases. Consequently, there is potential to create news feeds to legitimise the flow of content from multiple publishers, opening up opportunities for new revenues. Motivations exist to create more comprehensive and connected networks as a way to create relevance and future business models. It is less clear how to get regionals and nationals to step up in terms of economically redressing a balance that can fully sustain diverse and decentralised media supply chains even though improving the flow of content from communities is linked to the economic resilience of news business models more broadly. Stories that generate longer engagement are economically higher value. One regional manager said, "I think from a very high level you can draw a straight line from the eroding financial success of newspapers and their relevance to the community."

Acknowledgements

The Ping! platform was built as part of the Value My News project in collaboration with the University of Cardiff, the University of Central Lancashire, and Omni Digital between 2018 and 2020. Value My News was funded by Google Digital News Initiative with a technical extension called Ping! Trends funded by the Department for Culture Media and Sport, administered by the Future News Fund in 2020.

References

BBC. (2017) BBC announces media organisations which will employ Local Democracy Reporters as latest step in the Local News Partnerships. *BBC*. Available at: www.bbc.co.uk/mediacentre/latestnews/2017/local-democracy-reporters [Accessed 17 March 2021].

Bruns, A. (2014) Reconfiguring journalism: syndication, gatewatching and multiperspectival news. In (Ed.) Goggin, G. *Virtual nation the Internet in Australia*. Sydney: New South Publishing, pp. 177–192.

Cook, C. and Bakker, P. (2019) Viable, sustainable or resilient? *Nordicom Review* 40, pp. 31–49.

Cook, C., Geels, K. and Bakker, P. (2016) *Hyperlocal revenues in the UK and Europe: mapping the road to sustainability and resilience.* London: Nesta.

Copyright, Designs and Patent Act. (1988) *UK legislation portal* [Online]. Available at: www.legislation.gov.uk/ukpga/1988/48/contents [Accessed 10 February 2021].

Harte, D., Howells, R. and Williams, A. (2019) *Hyperlocal journalism: the decline of local newspapers and the rise of online community news.* London: Routledge.

Hern, A. (2020) New UK tech regulator to limit power of Google and Facebook [Online]. *The Guardian.* Available at: www.theguardian.com/technology/2020/nov/27/new-uk-tech-regulator-to-limit-power-of-google-and-facebook [Accessed 17 March 2021].

McLella, M. and Patel, M. (2011) *Getting local: how nonprofit news ventures seek sustainability.* Knight Foundation.

Ofcom. (2009) Local and regional media in the UK. *Ofcom.* www.ofcom.org.uk/research-and-data/tv-radio-and-on-demand/tv-research/lrmuk [Accessed 17 March 2021].

Omni Digital. (2020) Data driven product development for Value My News, VMN ping! news platform. *Omni Digital.* Available at: https://omni-digital.co.uk/case-studies/ping [Accessed 3 March 2021].

Pennycook, L. (2015) *Click and connect: case studies of innovative hyperlocal news providers.* Dunfermline: Carnegie Trust.

Ponsford, D. (2017) Independent declines to pay for court story "lifted" from Wales online telling freelance: "there is no copyright in news". *Press Gazette.* Available at: www.pressgazette.co.uk/independent-declines-to-pay-for-court-story-lifted-from-wales-online-telling-freelance-there-is-no-copyright-in-news/ [Accessed 20 December 2020].

Ponsford, D. (2017a) "David and Goliath" legal battle sees Rochdale Online win payout from Manchester Evening News over Danczuk expenses. *Press Gazette.* Available at: https://www.pressgazette.co.uk/david-and-goliath-legal-battle-sees-rochdale-online-win-payout-from-manchester-evening-news-over-lifted-news-story/ [Accessed 20 August 2021].

Radcliffe, D. (2012) *Here and now: UK hyperlocal media today.* London: Nesta.

Radcliffe, D. (2015) *Where are we now? UK hyperlocal media and community journalism in 2015.* London: Nesta.

Schaffer, J. (2007) *Citizen media: fad or the future of news.* J-Lab: The Institute for Interactive Journalism.

Tenor, C. (2017) *Hyperlocal news: after the hype.* Polis: London School of Economics.

Tobitt, C. (2019) Reach claims UK first as it tops 40m unique visitors across digital network. *Press Gazette.* Available at: www.pressgazette.co.uk/reach-claims-uk-first-as-it-tops-40m-unique-visitors-across-digital-network/ [Accessed 10 December 2020].

Williams, A., Barnett, S., Harte, D. and Townend, J. (2014) *The state of hyperlocal community news in the UK: findings from a survey of practitioners.* The Media Community and the Creative Citizen Project.

6 Community radio as citizen journalism

Aleksandar Kocic, Josephine Coleman, Jerry Padfield, and Jelena Milicev

Context

The collapse of local journalism has serious consequences for the health of democracy in both local communities and wider society. The public interest value of news is often viewed through the prism of its relationship to democracy (McNair 2009). Representative democracy enables good government most effectively if citizens' decisions are based on accurate and reliable information (Chambers and Costain 2001). In other words, journalism is a power for public good. This theoretical framework stems from normative democratic models of journalism (Hess 2017), especially the social responsibility model of the press (Hutchins 1947). As Mersey (2010) points out, journalism's connection to the public good derives from contemporary theories of the press, especially the social responsibility model, which underlies the watchdog role of journalism. In this way, journalists serve the political system by providing information, discussion, and debate on public affairs (Mersey 2010).

Understandings of what social or political purposes community radio is used for vary according to context. When community radio is framed as grassroots or locally – oriented media access initiatives predicated on a profound sense of dissatisfaction with mainstream coverage, then we can expect it to be dedicated to the principles of free expression and participatory democracy (Howley 2005: 2). This includes citizens being informed not just about what is going on at the national level, but also what happens in their local communities, as the latter is central to local engagement, participation, and social life (Wahl-Jorgensen 2019). This can be announcements of cultural and other events, interviews with local citizens, artists or volunteers, and, perhaps more importantly, the provision of "hard news".

Although a common term that many journalists understand instinctively, hard news is not easy to define. For Curran et al. (2010), hard news

DOI: 10.4324/9781003173144-7

is reports about politics, public administration, the economy, science, technology, and related topics. The more a news item is politically relevant, the more it reports in a thematic way, focuses on the societal consequences of events, is impersonal and unemotional in its style, the more it can be regarded as hard news (Reinemann et al. 2011: 233).

Local news provision has traditionally fallen to newspapers, with some regional-level television news from public service providers (BBC and ITV) and a patchy, thinly funded offer from commercial city-level TV stations (Youngs 2021). In England, radio has played a significant role in the provision of local news but more on a regional level, whereas in Scotland local public service radio never existed. Changes announced in 2020 and 2021 to the provision of regional radio news by the BBC seem contradictory, with an announcement of the merging of regional TV and radio news teams and "simplifications" to scheduling (BBC 2020; The Guardian 2020), followed nine months later by the announcement of six new local stations and new BBC local on-demand bulletins for over 50 areas (BBC 2021). In contrast to this expansion in England, the BBC considers that two dedicated national public service radio stations per devolved nation satisfy localised provision with some limited additions on an opt-out basis, such as those for Shetland and Orkney in Scotland. Commercial radio, while remaining popular, mostly offers syndicated national and international news in the form of hourly news bulletins produced by or based on the Independent Radio News service run by Sky News. Given the concerns highlighted by the Cairncross Review (Department for Digital, Culture, Media and Sport 2019) about a democratic deficit that may arise from the continued decline of the local press, can community radio help fill the local hard news provision vacuum?

Community radio

Community radio as a third tier of broadcasting arrived on the UK media scene relatively recently, with a pilot scheme launching in 2002 and the first stations awarded full-time licences going on-air from 2005. According to the UK media regulator Ofcom, a community station typically covers a small geographical area with a coverage radius of up to five km. Run on a not-for-profit basis, such stations can cater for whole areas or specific communities of interest – such as a particular ethnic group, age group, or interest group (Ofcom 2019). They are required to locally produce original material focused on catering for the informational needs, entertainment tastes, and cultural values of the target audiences to deliver social gain (Ofcom 2017). As of April 2021, there were 307 community radio stations, 31 of which were in Scotland, 16 in Northern Ireland, and eight in Wales (Ofcom 2021). In 2017, around 60% of the stations were aimed at listeners in a specific geographic area, with around 14% targeting minority ethnic communities, 10% youth, 7% community of interest, 5% religious, and 4% military (Lloyd 2018). Community stations are funded through grants, donations, commercial activities, and on-air advertising, with the latter capped at £15,000 or 50% of a station's annual income. The Government funding, established in the Communications Act 2003, is administered by Ofcom but stations apply with business plans for a share of the pot, which has stabilised at around £400,000.

While for some, the value and purpose of community broadcasting is located less in its broadcasting function and more in its community development function (van Vuuren 2002), our focus when looking at the "social gain" role of community radio is on its ability to deliver news to the community it serves. A recent survey by Coleman (2020a) finds that the majority of community radio teams do what they can to provide important information for their listeners. Most stations do not have a professional newsroom or experienced, trained journalists. On average, stations operate with 87 volunteers who together give around 209 hours of their time a week (Ofcom 2019). Some of them are "in-betweeners" (Ahva 2017: 2), since many have some industry experience. Local news provision is understood as interviews with community leaders, event organisers, or charity and business representatives on magazine-style shows where ongoing issues affecting the area are discussed. Some would even include "what's on" style announcements and summarising newspaper stories as local coverage (Coleman 2020b). Given the participatory nature of community radio broadcasting, what these practitioners produce amounts to a form of citizen journalism – news content produced by non-professionals (using the definitions in Wall 2015). It is also to some extent "hyperlocal journalism," although the term is normally used to describe web-based alternatives to professional media, which include citizen participation (Metzgar et al. 2011: 774). The conditions of hyperlocal media mean that expectations of them filling all legacy journalism's functions are unrealistic and, frankly, unjustified (Karlsson and Hellekant Rowe 2019) and this certainly applies to community radio in the UK.

In the remainder of this chapter, we outline practitioners' perceptions of the role UK community radio plays – or should play – in meeting the informational needs of the communities they serve. Through thematic analysis of interviews with station managers, we explore the experiences and perceptions of community radio volunteers with regard to local news provision and examine the adaptive strategies they employ to overcome challenges in providing local news.

Method

Semi-structured in-depth qualitative interviews with community radio station managers (n = 30) were conducted between June 2020 and February 2021 to gather data about the respondents' field of expertise and/or personal experience. A total of 24 participants were interviewed over the phone or via a videoconferencing platform and six via email. They were asked to provide details of their stations' key commitments, programming, funding, and strategies for the coverage of what Ofcom calls "community news and information" before and during the Covid-19 pandemic; specifically, we were interested in practitioners who interpreted that as the provision of hard news. Community radio stations were selected to include those that serve local geographical communities (n = 27) as well as those that serve communities of interest (n = 3). While all interviewees gave formal consent to being identified, in the interests of brevity, we identify stations only, so as to help readers look up stations of interest. The interviews were analysed using thematic analysis (see Braun and Clarke 2006).

Findings

Thematic analysis of our data revealed predominant perceptions of the role of community radio, the challenges in fulfilling it, and experiences in rising above these challenges. Three interconnected themes emerged: "local news provision as a moral duty," "challenges in local news provision," and "upping the game." This third theme consists of two subthemes, delineating different types of creative approaches to the said challenges: "automated news gathering" and "expanding and branching out." We explore each of these in turn in the following sections.

Local news provision as a moral duty

Interviewees insisted that there was a strong sense of purpose in providing a service for local communities. The station manager of *Nevis Radio*, a station that serves the small town of Fort William in Scotland, felt the station was relevant due to its "hyperlocal" offering: "That is what I consider a community radio – broadcasting information that people want, [and that] is entirely relevant to their street or their neighbourhood or their small village" (*Nevis Radio*). Being aware that they are increasingly the sole providers of community-orientated local content in many places seems to have elevated the sense of responsibility for this provision to the level of moral duty. In the case of *Switch Radio* in north-east Birmingham, they see other stations retreating from offering localised content:

> I think community radio stations – and I'd like to think that we've got this bit right – understand that there is a gap to be filled with local news and local content, because as others move away from that, there is a real opportunity there, and not necessarily just an opportunity in the selfish sense of, you know, more viewers, more readers, more listeners. I think there's a moral duty for community radio to fill that hole.
>
> (*Switch Radio*)

This sense of moral duty is particularly pertinent to the production of content that caters for the needs of specific subcommunities, such as the blind or the elderly, which are perceived to be at the heart of community radio:

> *The Talking Newspaper* has become a vital part of what we do. And initially you would argue that that's a very small, niche audience. But if we're not there to provide for small niche audiences at times then what are we there to do?
>
> (*Radio Verulam*)

> Nobody's doing just Belfast news that's relevant to the over 50s, you know, that service doesn't exist. I would just love there to be a truly local news service at the top, you know, a community news service sitting there. So that's a dream.
>
> (*Belfast FM*)

Challenges in local news provision

As mentioned earlier, income that community radio stations can raise through advertising is capped, which our respondents perceived as frustrating and hampering: "It'd be nice if our advertising wasn't capped. I understand why they do it. It's just, £15,000 is not much these days" (*Vectis Radio*). While some stations commended recently received grants, others spoke of additional challenges imposed by the pandemic: "Our finances have gone to the wall; we have very little advertising now" (*Celtic Music Radio*).

Lack of funding is one the key issues that prevents community radio from being more ambitious in news provision: "There is a definite appetite for local news, which people want freely available, however, without a way to monetise this content, it is difficult to meet these demands" (*Bute Island FM*). As a result, stations rely entirely on volunteers, implying that limitations in skill sets and availability may prevent community radio from performing its role as a hard news provider. This was highlighted by the manager of a Glasgow-based station dedicated to Scottish folk music and culture: "Training would be an absolute godsend for some of the kids we got. [...] Most people want to be disc jockeys but you gotta find those with other skills" (*Celtic Music Radio*).

Preferred news sources for the volunteers remain newspapers and "press releases from the County Council or the NHS or other bodies who want us to tell people something" (*Lionheart*). Also, stations do feel the pressure to meet regulatory standards while relying on untrained volunteers: "A lot of the stories that are from tabloid newspapers, we have to kind of de-sensationalise [...] because we want to stay on Ofcom's good side with these bulletins" (*CamGlen Radio*). For rural Scottish station *Bute Island FM*, finding volunteers is an issue:

> Our station is manned completely by volunteers, and we struggle for sufficient volunteers to fill our schedule at certain times, let alone asking for people to take on a news gathering role, and certainly we could not afford to take on salaried staff to fulfil this role.
>
> (*Bute Island FM*)

Upping the game

In their efforts to boost local news production, many stations have developed creative and innovative approaches with varying levels of success. However, some of those initiatives have not materialised due to the lack of enthusiasm by potential collaborators, as in the case of a station in Midlothian in Scotland looking to collaborate with a university journalism course.

> We did ask [for] a morning and afternoon bulletin from students but the [...] university seemed to shy away because staff would have to supervise even though *BDFM* would have been responsible for what goes on air.
>
> (*Black Diamond FM*)

Similarly, the station manager at *Crystal FM* in Scotland observed that community councils were "happy for us to promote what they do but reluctant to become involved in live or recorded broadcasting" (*Crystal FM*). Still, many other initiatives have had noteworthy responses and outcomes. Some stations resorted to cost-effective automated newsgathering, others to expanding their content and/or branching out into other platforms or establishing collaborations with institutions and newsmakers. We expand on each one of them in the following sections.

Automated newsgathering

Some stations have addressed shortages in funding and manpower by reverting to free online tools to gather news. *CamGlen Radio*, broadcasting to the outskirts of south-east Glasgow, for example, monitors search engines for key words relevant to their local areas and people of interest, such as politicians. Using Google Alerts, automated emails are delivered carrying information to supply content for news bulletins. *Paisley FM*, also near Glasgow, on the other hand, invites public institutions to email newsworthy information to the station, creating a pool of material from local and national governments, emergency services, utility companies, and such like. These strategies were not widely evident in our sample, but we highlight them as examples of commendable, cost-effective creativity.

Expanding and branching out

There seems to be an appetite for increased collaboration with the professional sector, linked to an increased confidence in stations' ability to provide quality local news coverage. *Switch Radio*, for example, uses freely available professional content supplied by the BBC-run Local Democracy Reporting Service (LDRS), praising it as a: "fantastic resource and godsend for [...] local news." Other managers have been in talks with local newspapers and retired professionals about possible collaborations in content creation.

> I've been in talks with the editor of one of the local papers, in fact a group of newspapers, about collaborating with them whereby they would feed us stuff and we would put together, you know, a local news bulletin which would go out, depending on what's in it, it would be recorded, and it would go on an automated basis until it's superseded. We've got all the technical stuff set up.
>
> (*Alive Radio*)

There's a chap at the county council who's due to retire and he wants to come and join us. And there's another retired journalist who wants to join us and in fact, another lady [...] who's a former *Daily Mail* online editor. [...] The newsroom would have to be voluntary. We're not in a position to pay anybody at the moment.

(*Wycombe Sound*)

Nevertheless, some stations are bravely expanding their own production with local election coverage, Q&As with local politicians, regular council-led slots, or programmes about Covid-related issues. Some stations are even venturing into other platforms, such as websites and podcasting, or the charmingly niche "knitcast" on *Source FM* in Cornwall, linking the audio content to a favourite listener pastime and "talking about local issues whilst knitting, which is a quite interesting thing" (*Source FM*).

We have a magazine show at the weekend called 'The Week', which discusses, sort of, either local news or national news with a local impact. So, that's a magazine show, so that's video and audio content. And we've just rebuilt our website to make that kind of stuff front and centre.

(*Switch Radio*)

Discussion

In this study, we explored station manager perceptions of the role of community radio in local news provision and their experiences in overcoming challenges in providing local news. Our thematic analysis resulted in three overarching themes emerging from the interviews.

Theoretical perspectives on the role of journalism outlined earlier demonstrate a clear need for robust local news provision in a democracy. The news media are critical to democratic governance as they provide a necessary (but perhaps currently not sufficient) ingredient for informed decision-making (Goidel et al. 2017). By serving as a public representative and watchdog over government performance, the media provide critical mechanisms for democratic accountability. After all, democracy functions best when its citizens are politically informed (Aalberg et al. 2010). Studies show that news media with high levels of political content affect knowledge and voter turnout positively (Althaus and Trautman 2008; Baekgaard et al. 2014). By reporting and commenting on current events, journalists help enhance popular sovereignty: they help citizens arrive at judgments about the common good (George 2013).

Community radio practitioners seem to understand this instinctively. We found that our interviewees regard it as their moral duty to assume the role of journalists and help to reverse the current downward trend in local news coverage using their links with local community as a strength. Local journalism increasingly faces the challenge not only of covering local affairs, but also of identifying what content resonates with their local audiences: what is local, and why the local is even relevant (Nielsen 2015). Community broadcasters come to radio with enormous enthusiasm for the medium and programme content, but they also bring a strong desire to serve their local community (Gordon 2015). A number of our interviewees even highlighted the need to serve niche communities at a local level – certain age groups such as those over 50 or disabled people. In this way, community radio in the UK embraces traditions from other countries that include genuine altruistic concern for unrepresented voices in the increasingly cacophonous public sphere (Starkey 2011).

Our research revealed some interesting initiatives, not all of them successful, on strategies to overcome the previously mentioned challenges. Attempts to link up with local authorities and politicians are mostly done on an ad hoc basis and are limited by volunteers' lack of training and resources as well as politicians' free time. Similarly, attempts to link up with journalism schools at UK universities are limited to personal initiatives and usually lack formal structures. More importantly, our data reveal that news provision efforts by community radio are often hampered by insecurities around regulatory requirements. This, on the one hand, tells us that there is an understanding of the regulatory framework, which requires the volunteer practitioners to conform with the Broadcasting Code (set out by the regulator, Ofcom, and covering standards in programmes, sponsorship, fairness, and privacy). The survey by Coleman (2020a: 5) shows that recruits who lack journalistic training and experience are introduced to the Broadcasting Code and encouraged to pursue professional standards in fact-checking and accuracy. However, this also raises an important question: is the current regulatory framework suitable for a voluntary sector and does it actually place the volunteers under a burden too heavy for them, given their lack of training in both journalistic skills and media law?

At the same time, we have come across interesting newsgathering practices that try to make the best out of limited resources and make up for the lack of skills and access to elite sources and institutions. These practices aim at reaching what is for many community stations still a distant goal – producing traditional news bulletins on a regular basis. It means that community stations seek to cover similar stories and turn to the same sources as their mainstream counterparts. This is in line with Coleman's (2020a) survey that shows that before the Covid-19 pandemic, local news was provided by community stations most commonly through on-air bulletins and shared online via social media, discussed on-air during magazine shows and posted on stations' websites. Most of the stations in Coleman's (2020a) survey also said they had been able to at least maintain this service, if not increase it, during the lockdown. But if the community sector is to play a more prominent role in local news coverage, additional funding models should be explored, including those that already exist in other countries (see Kocic and Milicev 2019). Some of this funding could then be targeted specifically at journalism training.

Conclusion

This chapter has highlighted community radio's approaches to local news provision and considered whether citizen journalists working for community radio can achieve professional standards. To qualify as journalism, the content needs to include some original interviewing, reporting, or analysis of events or issues to which people other than the authors have access (Nip 2006). This is why some argue that untrained citizens can only produce commentary, analysis, and opinion (Reich 2008) and are simply unqualified to produce original news content (Lemann 2006; Lowery 2006). Others claim that ordinary citizens can and should produce news (Allan 2006; Gillmor 2006), as, they are "learning how to join the process of journalism" (Gillmor 2006: XXV). While our data tell us that in many cases the ambition and effort are there, further research should evaluate the quality of the content produced and try to answer the question that Starkey (2011) asks: if required to depend disproportionately on volunteer talent, and unable to meet the expectations of "professionalism" in their output, will community stations lack credibility with their potential audience? For now, one way in which community radio can raise the quality (and quantity) of its journalistic output is through collaborations with professionals, as highlighted by our research. Formal and informal collaboration with "legacy" media organisations would also be a boost to volunteers' skillsets and confidence.

We acknowledge that the proposals outlined here present a starting point for discussion on the role of community radio in the provision of "hard news." Realistically, if local community broadcasters are to become part of the answer to the diminishing ability of the mainstream media to report on local affairs, there needs to be some structural adjustment. Further research should also look at the role of the regulatory framework – so that the expectations of the sector can be more clearly defined – as well as training schemes already in place or being considered. While the local news coverage by traditional media such as radio and newspapers is in decline, the evidence that new, digital forms of local media can sustain local journalism on a significant scale is inconclusive (Nielsen 2015). At the same time, radio in the UK is in good health and remains popular. Furthermore, the UK has, despite a late start, developed a vibrant community radio sector. Our research shows that when it comes to local news coverage, the volunteer radio sector certainly does not lack ambition or ideas. But to be able to turn those into professional-sounding news output, it needs better support.

References

Aalberg, T., van Aelst, P. and Curran, J. (2010) Media systems and the political information environment: a cross-national comparison. *International Journal of Press/Politics*, 15(3), pp.255–271.

Ahva, L. (2017) Practice theory for journalism studies: operationalizing the concept of practice for the study of participation. *Journalism Studies*, 18(12), pp.1523–1541.

Allan, S. (2006) *Online News*. Maidenhead: Open University Press.

Althaus, S.L. and Trautman, T.C. (2008) The impact of television market size on voter turnout in American elections. *American Politics Research*, 36(6), pp.824–856.

Baekgaard, M., Carsten J., Mortensen, P.B. and Serritzlew, S. (2014) Local news media and voter turnout. *Local Government Studies*, 40(4), pp.1–15.

BBC. (2020) *BBC announces cuts to English regional TV, radio and online output*. www.bbc.co.uk/news/entertainment-arts-53263793 (accessed on: 14 March 2021).

BBC. (2021) *BBC publishes blueprint for the biggest transformation in decades*. www.bbc.co.uk/mediacentre/2021/across-the-uk/ (accessed on: 25 March 2021).

Braun, V. and Clarke, V. (2006) Using thematic analysis in psychology. *Qualitative Research in Psychology*, 3(2), pp.77–101.

Chambers, S. and Costain, A. (eds.) (2001) *Deliberation, democracy, and the media*. Oxford: Rowman & Littlefield Publishers.

Coleman, J.F. (2020a) *UK community radio production responses to COVID-19*. London: Brunel University. Available at: http://bura.brunel.ac.uk/handle/2438/21156.

Coleman, J.F. (2020b) Situating Journalistic Coverage: A practice theory approach to researching local community radio production in the United Kingdom. In: Gulyas, A. and Baines, D. (eds.) *The Routledge Companion to local media and journalism*. London: Routledge, pp.343–354.

Curran, J., Salovaara-Moring, I., Cohen, S. and Iyengar, S. (2010) Crime, foreigners and hard news: a cross-national comparison of reporting and public perception. *Journalism*, 11(1), pp.3–19.

Department for Digital, Culture, Media and Sport (2019) *The Cairncross review: a sustainable future for journalism*. London: Department for Digital, Culture, Media and Sport.

George, C. (2013) Diversity around a democratic core: the universal and the particular in journalism. *Journalism*, 14(4), pp.490–503.

Gillmor, D. (2006) *We the media*. Sebastopol, CA: O'Reilly Media.

Goidel, K., Gaddie, K. and Ehrl, M. (2017). Watching the news and support for democracy: why media systems matter. *Social Science Quarterly*, 98(3), pp.836–855.

Gordon, J. (2015) The economic tensions faced by community radio broadcasters. In: Atton, C. (ed.) *The Routledge Companion to alternative and community media*. London: Routledge, pp.247–257.

Guardian. (2020) *BBC local news programming in balance due to budget cuts*. www.theguardian.com/media/2020/may/29/bbc-set-to-cut-regional-news-despite-high-audience-figures (accessed on: 14 March 2021).

Hess, K. (2017) Shifting foundations: journalism and the power of the 'common good'. *Journalism*, *18*(7), pp.801–816.

Howley, K. (2005) *Community media: people, places, and communication technologies*. Cambridge: Cambridge University Press.

Hutchins, R. (1947) *A free and responsible press: report of the commission on freedom of the press*. Chicago, IL: University of Chicago Press.

Karlsson, M. and Hellekant Rowe, E. (2019) Local journalism when the journalists leave town: probing the news gap that hyperlocal media are supposed to fill. *Nordicom Review*, 40(Special Issue 2), pp.15–29.

Kocic, A. and Milicev, J. (2019) Possible models of local news provision by radio in Scotland: a mixed-methods study. *Journal of Digital Media & Policy*, *10*(2), pp.183–201.

Lemann, N. (2006) Amateur hour: journalism without journalists. *The New Yorker*, 07.08. www.newyorker.com/magazine/2006/08/07/amateur-hour-4 (accessed on: 14 March 2021).

Lloyd, D. (2018) Small-scale radio in the UK: how local commercial and community radio can co-exist. *Radiocentre*. Available at: www.radiocentre.org/wp-content/uploads/2018/11/SMALL-SCALE-RADIO-IN-THE-UK-ONLINE.pdf (accessed on: 14 March 2021).

Lowery, W. (2006) Mapping the journalism – blogging relationship. *Journalism*, 7(4), pp.477–500.

McNair, B. (2009) Journalism in the 21st century—evolution, not extinction. *Journalism*, 10(3), pp.347–349.

Mersey, R.D. (2010) *Can journalism be saved? Rediscovering America's appetite for news*. Santa Barbara, CA: ABC-CLIO.

Metzgar, E.T., Kurpius, D.D. and Rowley, K.M. (2011) Defining hyperlocal media: proposing a framework for discussion. *New Media & Society*, 13(5), pp.772–787.

Nielsen, R.K. (2015) Introduction: the uncertain future of local journalism. In: Nielsen, R.K. (ed.) *Local journalism: the decline of newspapers and the rise of digital media.* London: Bloomsbury Publishing, pp.1–25.

Nip, J.Y. (2006) Exploring the second phase of public journalism. *Journalism Studies*, 7(2), pp.212–236.

Ofcom (2017) *Notes of guidance for community radio licence applicants and licensees.* Available at: www.ofcom.org.uk/__data/assets/pdf_file/0016/101860/Community-radio-guidance.pdf (accessed on: 14 March 2021).

Ofcom (2019) *Community radio.* Available at: www.ofcom.org.uk/manage-your-licence/radio-broadcast-licensing/community-radio (accessed on: 14 March 2021).

Ofcom (2021) *Community radio stations.* Available at: http://static.ofcom.org.uk/static/radiolicensing/html/radio-stations/community/community-main.htm (accessed on: 2 April 2021).

Reich, Z. (2008) How citizens create news stories. *Journalism Studies*, 9(5), pp.739–758.

Reinemann, C., Stanyer, J., Scherr, S. and Legnante, G. (2011) Hard and soft news: a review of concepts, operationalizations and key findings. *Journalism*, 13(2), pp.221–239.

Starkey, G. (2011) *Local radio, going global.* Basingstoke: Palgrave Macmillan.

Van Vuuren, K. (2002). Beyond the studio: a case study of community radio and social capital. *Media International Australia*, 103(1), pp.94–108.

Wahl-Jorgensen, K. (2019) The challenge of local news provision. *Journalism*, 20(1), pp.163–166.

Wall, M. (2015) Citizen journalism. *Digital Journalism*, 3(6), pp.797–813.

Youngs, I. (2021) Whatever happened to local TV? *BBC News.* Available at: www.bbc.co.uk/news/entertainment-arts-55854307 (accessed on: 25 March 2021).

7 Local data journalism practice in the UK

Jingrong Tong

Introduction

Data journalism is a form of journalism, telling stories in and from data (Tong and Zuo 2019). It is not a completely new form of journalism with its origins traced back to even the 18th and 19th centuries (Rogers 2013). Modern data journalism has gradually integrated into newsrooms in the UK from around 2008. Open (public records) data, which can be sliced according to geographical areas, offers opportunities for local journalism to address local issues and (re-)engage local communities. Data journalism is thus considered to be capable of reviving the role of local journalism in a democracy. However, local newsrooms' resource and skill deficiencies may prevent them from adopting and incorporating data journalism in their daily practice. This chapter examines how local data journalism is practiced within mainstream journalism in the UK. It outlines how local newsrooms gain support – from their parent company or external news organisations – for their data journalism practice, and how collaboration plays a key part in making local data journalism viable. It focuses on three collaborative models: by the data unit of Reach PLC (a UK national and regional newspaper publisher), the shared unit of the BBC, and the Bureau Local (a part of the Bureau of Investigative Journalism, a not-for-profit company funded primarily through philanthropic and grant funding). It also examines the contextual factors behind these practices and the challenges to their collaboration models' sustainability. The empirical data used comes from seven interviews with data journalists and editors at these three organisations (four from Reach, one from the BBC's shared unit, and two from Bureau Local), as well as an analysis of related data stories. With a particular focus on data journalism practice at the local level, the chapter contributes to the burgeoning literature, which usually focuses on data journalism practice at the national

DOI: 10.4324/9781003173144-8

level (see, for example, Knight 2015; Borges-Rey 2016, 2020; Granger 2019; Hurrell and Leimdorfer 2012).

The rise of data journalism in the UK and its context

The UK has been on the frontline of practicing modern data journalism; data reporting has become increasingly integrated into daily news reporting and institutionalised into the organisational structure of the national newsrooms (Borges-Rey 2016; Knight 2015; Tong 2020). Although the BBC began publishing school league tables online from as early as 1999 (Hurrell and Leimdorfer 2012), *The Telegraph's* and *The Guardian's* (2009) data stories such as the MPs' expenses scandal and *The Guardian*'s pioneering launch of its data store and accompanying *Datablog* signalled the start of systematically incorporating data journalism into daily reporting in UK newsrooms. National news outlets have since hired data reporters and assembled in-house data teams, usually small, with three or four members. Not limited to investigative reporting, data-driven stories can also be found in daily, short-form news stories with visual and interactive elements used to enhance audience engagement. During natural disasters or public health crises, data reporting has proved to be very useful. The coverage of COVID-19 in 2020 and 2021 by news media, for example, makes extensive use of data visualisation to help make sense of the story of the pandemic.

Data journalism in the UK has risen in the context of big and open data. Our society is deeply datafied, with our social lives increasingly recorded as quantified data (Mayer-Schönberger and Cukier 2013). Huge amounts of digital data coming from diverse sources are, therefore, constantly providing journalists and data scientists with resources to understand human activities. Another facilitating factor for data journalism is the emergence of the open data movement in 2007 (Chignard 2013). After Barack Obama's open government initiative in 2009, the British Government also launched its public records dataset (located at https://data.gov.uk), aimed at taking the transparency of governance to a new level. In the UK, the Freedom of Information Act (FOIA) was passed in 2000 and came into force in 2005. It gives citizens and journalists the right to request public records data from public authorities such as "printed documents, computer files, letters, emails, photographs, and sound or video recordings" (Information Commissioner's Office, no date). However, having such a right does not necessarily mean FOI requesters can access the data they request – requests may be rejected for reasons of privacy, confidentiality, and the costs for preparing the data exceeding the allowed cost limits.

Data journalism practice at the local level in the UK

In contrast to national newsrooms, which often dedicate their own data team to data reporting, local newspaper newsrooms mostly rely on the support provided by their parent company or other national news organisations to incorporate data journalism in their daily reporting. This section will discuss how three news organisations' collaboration models facilitate local data journalism practice in the UK.

Collaboration model one: in-house "data wire"

Reach PLC (previously Trinity Mirror) is the largest local newspaper publisher in the UK (Nilsson 2020) and home to 105 regional and local newspapers (as of January 2021) circulating in geographic areas across the UK. Since its Manchester-based data unit was launched in 2013, Reach PLC has run its own in-house "data wire" for its local titles within the company and has centralised the work of data reporting to the data unit. The two-member team in 2013 had grown to 12 in 2019, comprising data journalists, editors, coders, and graphic designers (Interview with Reach employee A, 28 February 2019). It was the first data journalism team within local news organisations (Granger 2019) which was then used as a template for the BBC's shared data unit (BBC 2020: 24). Later, launching their own data unit, JPIMedia and Newsquest, two other large regional media companies, adopted a similar model for their data journalism practice.

Reach PLC's data unit supports its local titles' daily reporting by providing them with the analysis of data dissected geographically. Based on their data analysis, data journalists produce and supply one or two localised "bulletins" each day, including "both news and sports" and text and video (Interview with Reach employee B, 15 April 2019). Many of these are about issues in the public interest, such as poverty and crime, education, and the NHS. However, it is down to local newsrooms to decide whether and how to use the stories:

> we write the stories and we write as many versions as possible … then we send them to the newsrooms, and it's up to them, whether they decide to publish them or not.
> (Interview with Reach employee C, 7 March 2019)

Upon receiving the stories from data journalists, journalists at local newsrooms may use them "straight away or added to with local reaction or case studies" (Interview with Reach employee B, 15 April 2019).

Usually, the data used for their stories is from open datasets held on the government's data store or obtained from government bodies through Freedom of Information requests. Apart from the daily, short data stories, the team also carries out long-term data projects, prominent among which are stories covering gender inequality, homelessness, and poverty. Collaborating with graphic designers and developers to create data-based interactives and infographics for newsrooms is also at the heart of the data unit's work. These interactives are often on topics in the public interest and/or in the interests of readers, such as "house prices, crime, GPs and hospital performance" (Interview with Reach employee B, 15 April 2019, also see further examples in Ottewell 2019).

Collaboration model two: providing "story packs" and training

Launched in 2017 and based in Birmingham as part of the BBC's Local News Partnerships project, the three-member shared data unit of the BBC supports data journalism practice in local newsrooms by providing them with data analysis and training to increase the data skills and knowledge of local reporters who are seconded to the unit for 12 weeks. Regularly, the unit prepares and shares with local newsrooms "story packs," containing the analysis of data collected from government open data or using other methods such as Freedom of Information requests along with the methodology for the analysis. From "story packs," local reporters can find local angles and develop stories for their audiences. Secondments are offered by the shared data unit three times a year to selected local reporters from their partnered local newsrooms. There are 12 places per year, lasting for 12 weeks. By 2020, 27 journalists had received training (BBC 2020: 8). The unit teaches secondees basic data, coding, and web scraping skills. A shared unit employee explained,

> over the course of three months, they learn how to analyse data, visualise data, and clean data. They learn advanced techniques such as programming language and free tools that they can use to analyse data. [...] And at the same time we get them working on data journalism projects as a collaborative initiative. [...] By the end of the three months when those journalists feel confident telling stories with data, they bring the learned data techniques back to their newsrooms.
> (Interview with the shared data unit employee, 29 March 2019)

During the COVID-19 pandemic, in-house secondments were changed to remote learning to suit the move to homeworking. "From September to October, 2020, the SDU ran a pilot with local news partners offering remote training sessions in four key areas. A total of 78 local journalists benefited from the sessions" (personal communication with Peter Sherlock, Associate Editor of Shared Data Unit 2021). The unit intends to nurture a collaborative culture among local newsrooms to soothe the challenges caused by financial and skill deficits (BBC 2020).

Collaboration model three: mobilising collaborations and networking

The Bureau Local, established in 2017, endeavours to mobilise close collaborations and establish a network with local and national newsrooms, experts, and citizen contributors. Providing resources to support local newsrooms to practice data journalism, it can also benefit from the local knowledge of local reporters to facilitate collecting data, conducting investigations, and setting agendas for nationwide debates on key issues such as domestic violence, the housing crisis, and deaths amongst the homeless community. In some cases, the Bureau Local comes up with an idea about an issue that they feel is important at the national level and needs to attract the nation's attention:

> Often we only take things that are systemic, … we won't take on individual stories, because we work at a national level, so we're looking at the systematic wrong, widespread wrongdoing or widespread public interest stories.
> (Interview with Bureau Local employee A, 13 November 2018)

Stories may also come from "a traditional tip-off or idea from a reporter but increasingly common and where we want to be surfacing stories, from local people through community organising" (personal communication with Megan Lucero, the Director of the Bureau Local, 23 April 2021). Local reporters, people, and those directly affected by issues are invited to join them in collecting experiences, data and conducting the investigation. They would also discuss with them which angle would be best for their respective audiences/readers.

Their collaboration model combines crowdsourcing, encouraging collaborations between local journalists, professionals such as technologists and experts/specialists who are close to or have knowledge of the issues under investigation, and citizens (Bureau Local, no date). Most of local journalists participating in their projects are "beat journalists" and occasionally "hyperlocal bloggers" (Interview with Bureau Local employee B, 26 March 2019). Since its launch in 2017 (to

2020), there have been 450 participants actively joining their network covering the whole country (Google News Initiative 2020). For example, in their homeless investigation, 11 network members participated, producing 95 local stories (The Bureau of Investigative Journalism 2020).

To summarise, the three news organisations offer three types of collaboration models that dominate local data journalism practice in the UK: collaboration between a data unit and beat journalists in local newsrooms within a big media company; collaboration between a national state news organisation and local news outlets; collaboration between a non-profit newsroom, local reporters, experts, and citizens. The next section discusses the values of these collaborative approaches.

Why collaboration?

Collaboration can be a route to help local newsrooms take up the opportunities offered by big data, open data, and data journalism. Like elsewhere in the world, UK news outlets have been dealing with their significant financial difficulties. In 2005, the UK had 1,286 local newspapers (Franklin 2007) but between 2005 and August 2020, more than 265 local titles were closed in the UK (Tobitt 2020a). Accompanying the prolonged financial difficulties faced by local newsrooms is the diminishing of local journalism and the crisis of quality news (Harte et al. 2018; Nielsen 2015; Tong 2020). The UK news media have been criticised for losing contact with local communities who are considered not to be adequately and appropriately represented by news outlets. The decline in local news supply is thought to be one of the most significant challenges journalism faces today (Wahl-Jorgensen 2019). In recognising the potential impact on local democratic engagement, in 2019, the UK Government invested £2 million to support local public interest journalism through Nesta's Future News initiative. However, its end report published in August 2020 (Sellick et al. 2020) shows that most of its funded innovators are journalism start-ups, new non-profit newsrooms, and small companies rather than traditional local newsrooms.

Under such circumstances, UK local newsrooms urgently need to find a solution to increase revenues and enlarge their audience base, to which practicing data journalism can contribute. However, not all local newsrooms and journalists can benefit from data reporting. The most prominent obstacle is lack of resources and skills. To practice data journalism properly, journalists would need to learn a wide range of skills (including programming and the use of specialist software). Although data journalism has become an elective option in the National Council for the Training of Journalists (NCTJ)'s Diploma in Journalism and some journalism schools have already started data journalism or computational journalism training, not all journalism schools have these types of courses. Updating curricula as well as the skills and knowledge of journalism educators and the existing journalism workforce takes time. Cash-strapped newsrooms may simply be unable to afford the investment needed for training or indeed allow their journalists sufficient time to carry out what can be time-consuming data journalism projects. By contrast, collaborating with an in-house data team or an external news organisation can give local newsrooms much-needed support, which enables them to tackle resources and skill shortages and to benefit from open data and the creative practices of data journalism.

The extent of collaboration-generated local data journalism coverage

At the time of writing (2021), the three collaboration models are successful in terms of generating local data journalism coverage. For the BBC's shared data unit, between 2017 and 2020, more than 1,000 news stories were produced from the unit's analysis in 31 data-driven investigations and published across multimedia platforms, including print, online, radio, and TV (BBC 2020 and personal communication with Peter Sherlock 2020).

The Nexis database (see Table 7.1) contains 436 news stories, published by UK local news outlets, which have used the research provided by the shared data unit (based on a search of local news stories containing the key words "the BBC" and "shared data unit" from 2017 to 2020). An analysis of these news stories reveals that over these four years, 171 news outlets used the shared data unit's analysis.

Table 7.1 Local news stories based on shared data unit research: 2017–2020

Year	Number of local news outlets using shared data unit's analysis	Number of news articles
2017	39	41
2018	72	126
2019	56	99
2020	87	170

Most of them were local newspapers owned by big commercial media companies such as JPIMedia, Newsquest, and Reach. The number of news articles published by local news outlets using the shared data unit's research increased from 41 in 2017 to 170 in 2020, though there was a decrease in 2019 due to a human resource shortage in the unit (Table 7.1). The topics of news stories are related to those in the public interest such as housing, crime, the NHS, the police, social benefits, and pollution. In 2020, the number of news stories increased significantly and their topics were mostly about COVID. Some of the reporters who used the shared data unit's analysis are actually data reporters such as Claire Miller and Annie Gouk of Reach. This indicates that in these cases, the shared data unit's research provided stories to data reporters from big news organisations such as Reach rather than increasing daily reporters' data reporting capacity. The unit's training and upskilling of local journalists has made an impact on local newsrooms. Two prominent examples of this are in 2019 with both JPIMedia and Newsquest launching data units following the training of reporters (Mayhew 2019; Granger 2019).

As for Reach PLC's data unit, it is valuable to focus on the work of one data journalist. The number of stories by the reporter, published by Reach's local titles and contained in the Nexis database from 2016 (soon after they joined the unit) to 2020, increased dramatically over time from 14 in 2016 to 589 in 2020 (Table 7.2). The big surge in the number of articles in 2020 is partly because of COVID-19. The data reporter's stories focused on children and young people, health and the NHS, abuse, social benefits, childcare, budget cuts and funding, the police and crimes, homeless and domestic abuse, schools, poverty, and workers' employment. The majority of the stories have the data reporter as the first or only by-line. Many of these stories have been localised, though some of them are similar or actually identical without being localised.

Table 7.2 Published news stories by the data reporter: 2016–2020

Year	Number of local news outlets using data unit's analysis	Number of news articles
2016	9	14
2017	17	42
2018	28	124
2019	35	288
2020	42	589

Table 7.3 News outlets using Bureau Local stories and stories published: 2017–2020

Year	Number of local news outlets using Bureau Local's research	Number of news articles
2017	28	39
2018	52	89
2019	57	90
2020	24	30

Altogether 54 local news outlets – about half of the news outlets owned by Reach PLC – used the data reporter's work in their coverage. Overall, *Manchester Evening News* (including *manchestereveningnews. co.uk*), which is based in the same city as the unit, was the top local newspaper that used the data journalist's 149 articles between 2016 and 2020, followed by *Liverpool Echo* (including *liverpoolecho.co.uk*) with 148 stories.

As for the Bureau Local, in the Nexis database, 248 news stories containing "Bureau Local," "the Bureau of Investigative journalism," or "Bureau of Local" were published by 102 UK local news outlets between 2017 and 2020 (articles on global topics related to the Bureau Global rather than Bureau Local were removed). The years 2018 and 2019 witnessed an obvious increase in the number of news stories but there was a decline in 2020 (see Table 7.3). The actual reasons for the decline are unknown, but one potential explanation (by the author) could be that local newspapers were hit hard by the pandemic and could not afford resources for extensive collaborations, as the Bureau Local has increasingly "seen the local news sector struggle which is why we are currently exploring how our shared model could be expanded on to help newsrooms survive and thrive" (personal communication with Megan Lucero 2021). *Eastern Daily Press* was the top local news outlet publishing 12 news stories about Norfolk using Bureau Local's research about farm pollution, domestic abuse, properties sold by councils, homeless, and cattle farming. Localising data stories is evident. The topic of homelessness was one of the most prominent in the dataset. Local news coverage containing the Bureau Local's research about homelessness peaked in 2018, slightly declined in 2019 and had a steep slump in 2020 (2017:3; 2018:36; 2019:22; and 2020:7). National newspapers such as *The Guardian*, *The Independent*, and *The Times* had much more extensive coverage using the Bureau Local's research than local newsrooms did.

The challenges to the sustainability of the three collaboration models

Despite the success of these collaborative models to date, challenges to their sustainability exist in three aspects: funding, collaboration, and resources. The challenges Reach PLC's data unit faces would be slightly different from the other two. As an in-house department dedicated to data journalism practice, its sustainability is down to the company's financial situation and strategies as well as local newsrooms' acceptance of data reporting. Profound financial deficits or low levels of acceptance and adoption of data stories by local newsrooms would lead to the demise of the data unit. The collaboration between data journalists and beat journalists depends on the extent to which beat journalists and local editors can recognise the value of data reports, find local angles, and allocate resources to make appealing stories for their local coverage. Their continuing success also depends on how committed the company is to data reporting, which is influenced by the availability of financial resources and the importance of data reporting recognised by the parent company. The growing number of the data journalists' news articles published by local newspapers is a good indicator for local newsrooms' continued and increasing acceptance of data reporting into their daily reporting. The importance of data to the coverage of COVID-19 has been a significant driving force behind the increase in the number of data stories. In addition, how much flexibility and time data journalists receive also influences the success of the unit in its ability to produce influential investigations and highly valued exclusives.

For the shared data unit of the BBC, the operational costs of the unit are covered by the annual funds – up to £8 million – invested by the BBC until the end of 2026 at least (Mayhew 2018). However, its sustainability is uncertain for several reasons. The looming threat to its operations first comes from the fact that the BBC itself is under great financial pressure. In 2020, for example, the BBC announced 450 job cuts in England with an aim to save £25 million by the end of March 2022 (Tobitt 2020b). The resource shortage in the shared unit itself also poses an immense challenge to its sustainability. In 2020, for example, there were only three core staff members: an associated editor, a senior journalist, and two journalists. Although they also work with secondees and other external experts, the major jobs of the operations of the data unit, such as partnership managements, preparing the story packs and managing the data hosted on the BBC website and GitHub (the collaborative shared software hosting and version control service), as well as providing training for trainee journalists, would go to the three members. It is challenging for the staff to deliver all the work. For example, the BBC admits that: "in 2019 the unit faced staffing and recruitment challenges that led to them being under-capacity for part of the year – which explains the slight dip in output" (BBC 2020: 18). It's also notable that most trainees seconded to the data unit are from big local news organisations, such as Reach, Newsquest, and JPIMedia rather than the smaller publishers. Modest news organisations may not be able to afford to release a journalist, who "might make up a third of the newsroom," to attend training for 12 weeks.

For the Bureau Local, grant funding is at the heart of its funding. Its initial funding ($660,000) came from the Google's Digital News Initiative, and since its launch, it has successfully secured new funds from other funders such as Open Society Foundations, Lankelly Chase, and the European Journalism Centre's Engaged Journalism fund. The Bureau Local stresses the importance of openness, collaboration, and engagement, yet it recognises the challenges posed by resources (Bureau Local 2019). The Bureau Local had four full-time employees plus a community organiser job share in 2019 with the number increased to seven full-time and two part-time roles in 2021 (personal communication with Megan Lucero 2021). Although this is a good sign, their resources are still modest for all the work ranging from building and running an extensive network to organising collaborative journalism projects and conducting investigations.

In terms of collaboration, a big challenge for Bureau Local is local newsrooms' support. For local newsrooms, resource limits but also the issue of exclusiveness would be an obstacle to participation. Different to the other two collaboration models where local newsrooms are sitting mostly at the receiving end of the data analysis provided by the data units, the collaboration model at the Bureau Local requires more, earlier-on, and active participation and collaboration from local newsrooms in the investigations. They also need to agree when their stories will be published. This proactive and extensive participation of local newsrooms in collaboration makes their support and recognition of the Bureau Local's work particularly important. Whether local newsrooms have resources for this is the significant challenge.

Conclusion

This chapter discusses three collaborative models in local data journalism practice in the UK. While they have achieved success, their sustainability is precarious. The precariousness comes from their own uncertain financial status but also local newsrooms' acceptance of data reporting and capability to make commitments to data reporting and collaboration. The financial challenge is real for all the three models though for the Bureau Local this situation is probably the most challenging as it largely depends on grant funding rather than institutional financial support. While grant funding enables journalism projects to happen, relying on grant funding is unreliable in securing a continuous, stable income. Funders such as Google may prioritise other societal issues over the future of local journalism in the UK. As for local newsrooms' acceptance and commitments, the data unit of Reach PLC has the most advantage for being the company's "in-house wire" and receiving support from both the BBC's share data unit and the Bureau Local, while the Bureau Local faces the biggest challenge for requiring closer collaboration. Overall, although the three collaboration models have made an impact, financial difficulties in the local news industry prohibit local newsrooms from making time and commitments to collaboration. The sustainable future of the three collaboration models requires an appreciation of the values of data reporting, which may take some while to nurture. Resource shortages would not help, as even if local newsrooms do value data reporting, they may not have the capacity to fully benefit from it.

References

BBC. (2020) *A Review of the BBC Local News Partnership*. Available at: https://downloads.bbc.co.uk/aboutthebbc/reports/reports/lnp-review-2020.pdf (accessed 25 March 2021).

Borges-Rey, E. (2016) Unravelling Data Journalism. *Journalism Practice*, 10(7), pp.833–843.

Borges-Rey, E. (2020) Towards an Epistemology of Data Journalism in the Devolved Nations of the United Kingdom: Changes and Continuities in Materiality, Performativity and Reflexivity. *Journalism*, 21(7), pp.915–932.

Bureau Local. (2019) *Let's Talk About Sustainability: The Bureau Local's Approach to Business Development*. Available at: https://docs.google.com/document/d/13Md1nr_JcOi7UM2wx7tO3cWzNpJVhm9NyIUUdIDYJsk/edit (accessed 25 March 2021).

Bureau Local. (no date) *About Bureau Local*. Available at: www.thebureauinvestigates.com/explainers/about-the-project (accessed 25 March 2021).

Chignard, S. (2013) A Brief History of Open Data. *Paris Tech Review*. Available at: www.paristechreview.com/2013/03/29/brief-history-open-data/ (accessed 25 March 2021).

Franklin, B. (2007) Attacking the Devil? Local Journalists and Local Newspapers in the UK. *In:* Franklin, B. (ed.) *Local Journalism and Local Media: Making the Local News*. London: Taylor & Francis, pp.3–15.

Google News Initiative. (2020) *The Bureau Local*. Available at: https://newsinitiative.withgoogle.com/dnifund/dni-projects/bureau-local/ (accessed 25 March 2021).

Granger, J. (2019) BBC Shared Data Unit Inspires Data Journalism Teams Across the UK to Collaborate on Public Interest Stories. *journalism.co.uk*. Available at: www.journalism.co.uk/news/how-the-bbc-shared-data-unit-is-inspiring-data-units-across-the-uk/s2/a747677/ (accessed 25 March 2021).

Harte, D., Howells, R. & Williams, A. (2018) *Hyperlocal Journalism: The Decline of Local Newspapers and the Rise of Online Community News*. London: Routledge.

Hurrell, B. & Leimdorfer, A. (2012) Data Journalism at the BBC. *In:* Gray, J., Bounegru, L. & Chambers, L. (eds.) *The Data Journalism Handbook*. Sebastopol, CA: O'Reilly Media, pp.28–31.

Information Commissioner's Office. (no date) *Public Authorities under the Freedom of Information Act*. Available at: https://ico.org.uk/media/for-organisations/documents/1152/public_authorities_under_the_foia.pdf (accessed 25 March 2021).

Knight, M. (2015) Data Journalism in the UK: A Preliminary Analysis of form and Content. *Journal of Media Practice*, 16(1), pp.55–72.

Mayer-Schönberger, V. & Cukier, K. (2013) *Big Data: A Revolution that Will Transform How We Live, Work and Think*. Boston, MA and New York, NY: Houghton Mifflin Harcourt.

Mayhew, F. (2018) One Fifth of BBC-Funded Local Democracy Reporter Roles Still to be Filled Six Months on, but Scheme Said to be 'Progressing Well'. *PressGazette*. Available at: www.pressgazette.co.uk/one-fifth-of-bbc-funded-local-democracy-reporter-roles-still-to-be-filled-six-months-on-but-scheme-said-to-be-progressing-well/ (accessed 25 March 2021).

Mayhew, F. (2019) Newsquest Launches Data Investigations Unit with Three BBC-Trained Reporters. *PressGazette*. Available at: www.pressgazette.co.uk/newsquest-launches-data-investigations-unit-with-three-bbc-trained-reporters/ (accessed 25 March 2021).

Nielsen, R.K. (ed.) (2015) *Local Journalism: The Decline of Newspapers and the Rise of Digital Media*. London and New York, NY: I.B. Tauris.

Nilsson, P. (2020). UK Newspaper Publisher Reach to Cut 550 Jobs. *The Financial Times*, 7 July 2020.

Ottewell, D. (2019) One Data Journalist, One (Big) Spreadsheet … the Data Journalism Project Which Grew and Grew. *Behind Local News*. Available at: https://medium.com/behind-local-news-uk/one-data-journalist-one-big-spreadsheet-the-data-journalism-project-which-grew-and-grew-4454e003e3e8 (accessed 25 March 2021).

Rogers, S. (2013) John Snow's Data Journalism: The Cholera Map That Changed the World. *The Guardian*.

Sellick, V., Newman, I., Hamilos, A., et al. (2020) *Future News Pilot Fund: End of Programme Report*. London: Nesta, DCMS, Bethnal Green Ventures.

The Bureau of Investigative Journalism. (2020) *Homelessness: A Project Counting the Human Costs of Homelessness*. Available at: www.thebureauinvestigates. com/projects/homelessness (accessed 25 March 2021).

The Guardian. (2009) *Welcome to the Datablog*. Available at: www.the guardian.com/news/datablog/2009/mar/10/blogpost1 (accessed 25 March 2021).

Tobitt, C. (2020a) UK Local Newspaper Closures: At Least 265 Titles Gone since 2005, but Pace of Decline Has Slowed. *PressGazette*. Available at: www.pressgazette.co.uk/uk-local-newspaper-closures-at-least-265-local-newspaper-titles-gone-since-2005-but-pace-of-decline-has-slowed/ (accessed 25 March 2021).

Tobitt, C. (2020b) BBC England to Cut 450 Jobs Across TV, Radio and Online as £25m Savings Needed in Two Years. *PressGazette*. Available at: www.pressgazette.co.uk/bbc-england-to-cut-450-jobs-across-tv-radio-and-online-as-25m-savings-needed-in-two-years/ (accessed 25 March 2021).

Tong, J. (2020) Paradigm Reinforcing: The Assimilation of Data Journalism in the UK. *Journal of Applied Journalism and Media Studies*. DOI: 10.1386/ ajms_00043_1.

Tong, J. & Zuo, L. (2019) The Inapplicability of Objectivity: Understanding the Work of Data Journalism. *Journalism Practice*, 15(2), pp.153–169.

Wahl-Jorgensen, K. (2019) The Challenge of Local News Provision. *Journalism*, 20, 163–166.

8   Considering slow local news

Mark Dunford

Understanding the local

Nick Davies (2008) draws attention to structural weaknesses of the news media where the pressure to reduce costs, increase revenue, and operate within a 24-hour news cycle has undermined the integrity of journalism. He highlights an uncritical dependency on material gathered through news agencies, especially the Press Association that is "honest in intent, efficient in performance, cost effective as a business – and, I believe entirely inadequate for the role in which it has now been cast" (2008: 75). He focuses on the pressures placed on an under-resourced organisation that lacks the capacity needed to cover anything beyond "its mainstream supply of home news stories" (2008: 76). He laments the declining use of local correspondents and thus a decline in local news provision that is very much still ongoing. Research completed by the Press Gazette in 2018 reported the loss of 245 local news titles between 2005 and 2018 with the loss of 275 editorial jobs in 2018 alone (Mayhew 2019). Matthews (2017) chronicles a process of decline characterised by a loss of revenue and a concentration of ownership so that by 2016, 78 per cent of provincial news titles were in the hands of just four companies.

Davies' greatest criticism is, however, levelled at the use of material provided by public relations (PR) agencies that have filled the gap created by the pressures across the media, especially at the local level. Davies acknowledges PR is not a new concern, he points to the role of PR companies across different sectors to press a particular case and uses the example of the US tobacco industry in the 1950s to show how dubious material can be given credibility by authoritative PR (2008: 157–204). Pressures on news providers have, however, reduced the scope for critically interrogating PR and there are many examples of press releases being presented as impartial news. This uncritical recycling of

DOI: 10.4324/9781003173144-9

PR material was originally referred to as Churnalism in 2006 and was of sufficient concern to the Media Standards Trust that in 2011 they established a website, *churnalism.com*, designed to both verify the use of PR material in stories and to draw attention to the phenomenon. Lewis et al. (2008: 18) draw on a sample of 2207 home news stories from five selected titles to interrogate the relationship between journalism and PR and conclude that in a constrained organisational setting, where the scope for effective journalism is curtailed, PR "will favour those, notably business and government, best able to produce strong and effective PR material" (14).

A different approach

Slow journalism is a complex, difficult, and contested term describing a contrasting approach to journalistic practice. It occupies a space where time is taken to craft a carefully written, reflective piece exploring the underlying causes and consequences of a particular event or subject rather than the immediate effects. In this respect, it offers a slow-paced alternative to a deadline-driven form of daily journalistic practice. The quarterly magazine *Delayed Gratification*, the pioneer of self-conscious slow journalism, was first published in the UK in 2011. Other publications have followed a similar approach, notably *Tortoise Media* launched in 2019 with significant online presence and a cast of experienced writers drawn from mainstream news organisations. Niche publications have addressed specific markets. For example, the US-based subscription-only website *The Athletic* launched in the UK during 2018 with a particular focus on football and a mix of lengthy articles and regular podcast output. Much slow journalism is now online where costs are low. Locally based or subject-focussed subscription models include the resolutely independent music publication *Loud and Quiet* that has steadily built up a membership base through the bimonthly magazine and an accompanying set of playlists, merchandise, and special offers for featured music.

Jennifer Rauch (2018) traces the history and inspirations driving slow media. Taking inspiration from different sources, she describes how the slow food movement started in Italy during the mid-1980s and rapidly spread across the globe to inspire a deeper consideration of the relationship between quality, locality, and identity across a range of different sectors, including the media. The proliferation of farmers markets showcased the power of localised supply chains and thereby highlighted the personal connections between production and consumption. Slow food inspired slow media with an emphasis on careful preparation and a focus on the right ingredients that initially manifested itself in a preference for print and analogue over digital. Slow media spawned slow journalism as a reaction to the pace and volume of activity generated by the pressures of the 24-hour digital news cycle. Rauch identifies "seven layers of meaning" (2018: 37) or characteristics inherent within slow journalism, namely that it should be seen to be slow – "journalism that enacts a critique of live reporting and the culture of speed," (ibid.) – investigative, selective, narrative based, fair, community orientated, and participatory. Rob Orchard, the editor of *Delayed Gratification*, has argued that contemporary journalistic practice lacks accuracy, impartiality, context, and depth (Orchard 2014). He draws attention to the factors driving this – the closure of titles, the loss of reporters, and a fall in revenues across the news landscape – and speculates about a spiral of decline where resources for journalism dwindle. He calls for a "slow journalism revolution" (ibid.), stressing the development of a thoughtful perspective over-simplistic, fast reactions, and prioritises the importance of context as a means to build a more considered or holistic understanding.

Working to realise the ambitions set by Rauch and Orchard is easier said than done. The tools of the journalistic trade are long established and accompanying commercial pressures may well restrict the immediate scope for innovation to publications where advertising or subscriptions ensure financial viability. Having said this, it is possible to imagine the opening up of local media where the impetus is driven by a public service ethos, such as that defined by the Cairncross Review (Department for Digital, Culture, Media and Sport 2019), a point where local media is able to rectify a political and cultural loss through the creation of a different media space. In his discussion of Hauntology, the cultural theorist Mark Fisher challenges us to imagine a future "whose threatened coming was already playing a part in undermining the present state of things" (2014: 6). Matthews (2017) explores the social value and civic importance of a local and regional news provision dependent on area-based journalistic skills, knowledge, and expertise. Ian Hargreaves and John Hartley (2016) suggest different interventions that could be used to help extend viable local media provision. These range from direct subsidy via partnerships with the BBC (as discussed in the introduction to this book) or local authorities, through to the provision of grant funding from the National Lottery, the hypothecation of funding derived from a tax on social media giants, or an exemption from VAT. Any, or all, of these could be used to address the questions of financial sustainability that bedevil considerations of local media provision. Though funding and resourcing are clearly a critical concern, it doesn't provide a direct address to the question of content. A better funded and resourced local media provision that succeeds by simply using recycling existing forms of content to provide an alternative media source runs the risk of being squeezed out of a competitive market, along the lines of the local coffee shops that lose out to the predatory, chain operators.

One possible way to imagine a different local media landscape is to consider the nature of content within local media and to explore whether modes of production that utilise different means of creating content that address Rauch's "layers of meaning" (2018: 37) might provide a more viable, sustainable model. Slow Journalism offers one possible route and there could be real value in balancing slower, more deliberative forms of localised storytelling alongside deadline driven, fast news provision. As local newsprint media continue to decline and shiftonline, it is hard to conceive of a financially viable text-based local media. Therefore, different forms of content will be needed if a sustainable model is to be realised, including audiovisual material, infographics, and interactive. Without this, there will, as Cairncross warned, be a diminished public space. It is possible to draw inspiration from slow media as a means to envisage a more deliberative and contemplative form of local media that provides scope for a means to provide a deeper consideration of events and issues, yet the question around localised content remains: where does material come from and how is it sourced?

Voice

The exploration of voice by Nick Couldry starts with the assertion that "we are experiencing a contemporary *crisis* of voice, across political, economic and cultural domains, that has been growing for at least three decades" (2010: 1, emphasis in the original). He argues that voice is both a process and a value – the former being the act of providing an account and the latter being a way of thinking about social, political, and cultural organisation that enable voices to be raised and heard: "the commitment to *voice that matters*" (2010: 3, emphasis in the original). He goes on to identify new possibilities for voice enabled by new technologies – namely scope for new voices within public discourse, an increase in mutual awareness of these new voices, new scales and modes of organisation of these voices, the changing nature of our understanding of the spaces required for a conversation, and the scope for all these changes to generate new, more intense forms of listening. For local media, these new possibilities could add a shape and purpose to a reconceptualisation but they need to be realised in a way that both enable a process for voices to be raised and places a social, political, and cultural value in spaces where they can be heard. Local news media should be a space in the digital sphere where Couldry's ambition is at least partly realised, one where local issues are identified, debated, and resolved.

In *Ghosts of my Life*, Mark Fisher draws on Derrida to use the idea of hauntology to interrogate and extend an understanding of that which has been lost in the past, but also "that which, in actuality, has *not yet* happened, but which is *already* in the virtual (an attractor, an anticipation shaping current behaviour)" (2014: 19, emphasis in original). Both haunt the present. Possible future hauntings are often positioned as negative or dangerous – for example, the global terror threat – and these can often be driven by specific political positions or cultural fears. For Fisher, the present is therefore shaped by the past, and what has been lost in the shaping of it, but also by a closing down of possibility. His writing is challenging readers to imagine a different future, one where the possibilities in the present can realise different outcomes.

Reclaiming lost content

For this to occur within the context of local media provision, content needs to be reconsidered and thought needs to be given to what has been lost, why it has gone and how it can be replaced. An under-resourced local media culture that is dependent on quick turnaround reporting and PR for content offers little scope for investigative reporting or reflection. While Hargreaves and Hartley (2016) engage directly with the question of provision, they fail to interrogate the issue of content; of who speaks, what is said, and where the audience is. For Couldry (2010), these are the key issues, yet the question around how to address them within the context of local media provision has yet to be explored. The characteristics of slow media, as identified by Rauch, could be adapted to offer a way to understand what could become a comparable set of desirable features for aspects of local media provision, namely local news could be deliberately slow, investigative, selective, narrative based, fair, community orientated, and participatory. There needs to be a way to conceive of different forms of content within local news so that the possibilities are realised. One way to achieve this would be to draw on the methodologies used widely within participatory media by practitioners and researchers, namely digital storytelling, photovoice, and participatory video. Each of these offers a different digital possibility and all provide a means to engage productively with Rauch's layers of meaning.

Digital storytelling

Digital storytelling is a widely used term to describe an array of creative activities used in different settings. Lundby (2008: 1) points to its use to describe visual effects or the creative potential in interactive entertainment. It is, however, specifically used to refer a simple creative process where people with little or no experience of digital technology or creative practice, gain the skills needed to tell a two-minute personal story using predominantly still images combined with their own recorded voice over. Stories are ordinarily self-representational short films and emerge from a collaborative process known as a story circle, in which a range of stimuli are used to develop trust across of group of eight or so participants as means to find a story each of them can tell with confidence. The approach developed from work begun at the StoryCenter in Berkeley, US in 1994 and its founder Joe Lambert sets out different methodological approaches to digital storytelling in his Digital Storytelling Cookbook (Lambert 2010). As of 2021, there is an established and growing network of digital storytelling practitioners and researchers across the globe and digital stories are widely used for academic research, advocacy, or community consultation as a means to engage young people or "hard to reach" communities (see examples in Dunford and Jenkins 2017; Hartley and McWilliam 2009).

The storytelling aspect of digital storytelling and the potential within it has grown to dominate critical discourse around the practice. Large numbers of stories have been made but as Hartley (2013) points out, stories require both a narrator and a receptive audience, something digital stories have routinely struggled to find. He challenges those interested in digital storytelling as a practice to "scale up from self-expression to communication" (2013: 71) and to explore ways in which the practice can reach beyond a limited audience to inform a wider polity. The production processes within digital storytelling share much with Rauch's slow media, that is, a commitment to reflection, narrative, and participation as means to understand communities and the dynamics within them. For nearly three decades, digital storytelling has struggled to find a receptive media space providing it with the willingness and means to reach an audience. To establish meaning, stories need to be curated or contextualised within specific framings. Prominent among recent examples working to address this is the Story Mapping initiative (see http://wp.story-mapping.org) established by Joe Lambert at *StoryCenter* that uses mapping software as a means to geo-locate stories and provide a specific account of a place or community within it. There are a number of potentially different but complementary components to Lambert's work. At a basic level, the approach has the potential to provide a psychogeographic account of an area but this can be extended to activism so that it chronicles community development or records moments of resistance.

Individual digital stories have also been used by specific media outlets. For example, the *Seattle Times* used a digital story told by Maria Blancas as the basis for an article describing her experience as a child of immigrant farmworkers and her subsequent journey to become a prize-winning PhD student (Shapiro 2019). Her digital story is embedded at the end of the article. A comparable approach with a greater emphasis on activism was taken in Denver where the *Denver Post* reported on a workshop organised by the *Center for Digital Storytelling* (later to be called just *StoryCenter* from 2015). In the workshop, individuals told stories of their passion and commitment to civil and human rights (Martin 2013) although in this example the newspaper simply reports on the workshop and offers a chance to enrol in subsequent activity, rather than providing links through to the individual stories that could have added the context and depth to a revised report. In the UK, *Curiosity Creative's* community-based digital storytelling work in Newcastle was featured on BBC's Look North (broadcast 20 August 2017) as an example of place-based community engagement filmmaking with interviews featuring local storytellers talking about the power of the process and a showcase for a "pop up" local exhibition in community settings.

The most well-known example of a broadcaster using digital storytelling is *Capture Wales/Cipolwg ar Gymru*, an initiative run by BBC Wales from 2001 through to 2008 which saw the production and broadcast of hundreds of digital stories made through a partnership with different community groups across Wales as part of the BBC's *Connecting with Communities* initiative. All the *Capture Wales* stories and the supporting material were deposited in the National Library of Wales when the initiative closed in 2008. These stories are primarily short, personal reflections told in a distinctive style that is rooted in community arts practice. Taken together they provide a complex, unfolding portrait of Wales that makes a distinctive contribution to its contemporary social history. They were broadcast on the BBC and questions around the self-representation of communities through *Capture Wales* have been widely explored (Thumim 2012; Lewis and Matthews 2017). By broadcasting these stories after the early evening news in the prime-time schedule and distributing them on the website, the BBC was able to be seen to be working to extend "the range and type of representation that appeared on the platforms of broadcast institutions" (Thumim 2012: 100). These stories were restricted to short documentary-style self-representations by the digital storytelling form and the community-based storytelling practices associated with it. Stories were actively told by the makers and therefore enabled new voices to be heard within public discourse. To this extent, *Capture Wales* engaged actively with ambitions set by Couldry (2010). These snapshots and the earlier examples suggest how a more grounded form of digital storytelling could be used as means to develop slow, community focussed, participatory journalistic practices that could be integrated constructively into existing media platforms.

Photovoice

Photovoice offers a different approach to community-orientated participatory work. It involves providing marginalised people or communities with cameras and then training people to use them before asking them to use the camera to visually document their own lived experience. Any type of camera may be used, but, given the emphasis on accessibility and speed, it is often simplest to use basic cameras or even widely available camera-equipped mobile phones. Participants are ordinarily provided with a prompt or question to structure their storytelling. Elaine Bell Kaplan's *We Live in the Shadow: Inner City Kids tell their stories through photographs* (2013) provides a clear account of the photovoice process she led with young people in south central Los Angeles. She sets out a process of training in basic photographic techniques and then simply passes cameras to young people so they can photograph their everyday lives. The resulting material is then gathered together and categorised to tell the story of young people's lives through their own eyes as they experience education, family, and neighbourhood life across the inner city. Interviews with the participants are included with the images to complete an anthropological documentary process. Her ambition is to use the photovoice method as a means to raise awareness and so that lives that would otherwise be absent are seen and voices are heard. In the UK, the charity *PhotoVoice* uses the methodology as part of its social change mission. Recent work (at time of writing) includes *Care Leavers in Focus (CLiF)*, a three-year initiative where participants use photography "as a tool for advocacy and self-expression" (PhotoVoice 2021). Through a collaboration with national policy makers, representative organisations, and local authorities, *PhotoVoice* is using this participatory methodology as a consultation tool so it can influence policy and shape the future delivery of services. In this example, the ambition and the link between the participatory practice and the intended outcome are built into the design of the project and the charity is acting as a conduit to connect different worlds. Claudia Mitchell et al. (2017) stress the potential usage of photovoice and other participatory visual research methodologies as a vehicle to connect "hard to reach" people directly to policy makers. Photovoice is a relatively simple, low-cost process that provides a means for voices that would otherwise be lost to be heard by a policy making audience.

Participatory video

Participatory video offers a third distinctive, yet overlapping, methodological approach to participatory media production that could be utilised as a slow form of local media practice. Like digital storytelling and photovoice, it starts from the premise that media production has grown progressively simpler and more accessible. This makes it possible to bring together groups of marginalised people to help them tell stories of immediate concern to them and their communities that can be actively used as the basis to address specific subjects or problems. Andy Porter (2007) charts his own filmmaking experiences and the use of different labels across three decades of activist-based filmmaking, variously described as alternative, community, radical, grassroots, underground, or tactical. His work consistently held "a belief in the importance of people being able to create and control the production of their own images and messages and get them seen and heard in the world" (2007: 74). His own community-based work in North Kensington, London explored different approaches to participatory media, including the *News at W10* in 1974 that used a magazine format to provide a locally distributed form of community television news. Participatory video is focussed on community empowerment where the production company works to facilitate the identification of issues that are subsequently addressed in the film. Authorship is firmly placed in the hands of the community. Nick Lunch and Chris Lunch (2006) trace the roots of participatory video practice through to the work of Canadian filmmaker Dan Snowden. His 1967 work with villagers on the Fogo Islands off the coast of Newfoundland highlighted commonalities between remote villagers. This initiated a dialogue between the villagers and government that led directly to policy change that improved local lives. Participatory video is now used as a community-based consultative tool or a means of advocacy to establish depth, context, and understanding of indigenous communities around the world. In 2019, the Global Anti-Corruption Team at *Transparency International* worked with 11 local people from the Gambia to create Hyena, a film charting human rights abuses under the 22-year dictatorship of Yahya Janneh (see www.equals.org.uk/corruption-human-rights). In addition to being submitted as evidence to the Truth, Reconciliation and Reparations Commission (TRRC), this was subsequently shown on *QTV* and *Star TV* and, at the time of writing, further participatory video projects have been commissioned to explore issues around corruption.

The participatory video production process has since evolved and adapted to meet the challenges of different settings, the impact of digitalisation, and the distribution potential of the internet. It has, for example, been taken forward by *People's Voice Media* in Manchester whose work uses participatory video as a community development tool to build skills and establish dialogue driven by voices that are ordinarily marginalised in media production. Their work stretches across different sectors to embrace health, social care, and heritage, as well as training designed to address digital exclusion. The particular emphasis within it on a structured approach to community reporting centred on the gathering, curation, and mobilisation of stories provides an example of how digital technology has enabled participatory video practices and extended the collection of stories without routinely extending the sharing of stories beyond a localised activist, policy making, or academic base. However, criticism levelled by Hartley (2013) at digital storytelling is equally valid for participatory video practice or photovoice, in the sense that the work is not widely seen.

Conclusions

The challenges facing the local media landscape are immense. Titles have closed, journalists have lost their jobs and the veracity of content has been undermined by the combined forces of PR and commercialism as sales have fallen and advertising income has shifted online. The local polity has been diminished by both a loss of voice and an absence of opportunities for voices to be listened to. The opportunities for the possibilities of voice enabled by new technologies suggested by Couldry (2010) have yet to be realised at a local level. Voices may be raised but they are rarely heard by a large audience. Fisher's work (2014) challenges us to balance an understanding of the past, the present, and the future, to explore the different dimensions within this. By looking carefully at what has been lost, we can better understand the forces shaping the present and see what might be missing in the future.

Slow journalism and slow media flourish in media spaces where particular subjects, such as music or sport, or particular approaches to news, hold sway over the immediacy of content. They offer examples of how different ways of engaging with an audience, through, for example, building a membership base, can open up scope for viable new media. Each of these addresses the seven layers of meaning inherent in slow media identified and explored by Rauch (2018). Yet slow journalism and slow media drew inspiration from the slow food movement, a localised phenomenon. This was partly achieved by offering different forms of produce or content. One way to conceive of slow local news and media is to draw on this and to look for different approaches to storytelling or newsgathering as a means to reimagine the media landscape. The possibilities offered by established participatory media forms – which clearly resonate with slow media characteristics – offer a potential means to provide new, slower content for local news providers that provide representative accounts of communities and their concerns. They are, however, also currently focussed on life stories, advocacy, and training, so to succeed as viable local media they would need to shift to away from an issue-based approach to one that could provide a credible journalistic account of place that resonates with local audiences as being sustainable, accurate, and impartial. In this respect, there is scope to draw on these approaches as a means to realise the possibilities that enable us to move towards a slow local news.

References

Bell Kaplan, E. (2013) *We Live in the Shadow: Inner City Kids Tell Their Stories through Photographs.* Philadelphia, PA: Temple University Press.

Couldry, N. (2010) *Why Voice Matters, Culture and Politics after Neoliberalism.* London: Sage.

Davies, N. (2008) *Flat Earth News.* London: Vintage.

Department for Digital, Culture, Media and Sport. (2019) *The Cairncross Review: A Sustainable Future for Journalism.* London: Department for Digital, Culture, Media and Sport.

Dunford, M. and Jenkins, T. (2017) *Digital Storytelling Form and Content.* London: Palgrave Macmillan.

Fisher, M. (2014) *Ghosts of My Life.* London: Zero Books.

Hargreaves, I. and Hartley, J. (2016) *The Creative Citizen Unbound: How Social Media Contribute to Civics, Democracy and Creative Communities.* Bristol: Policy Press.

Hartley, J. (2013) A Trojan Horse in a Citadel of Stories? Storytelling and the Creation of Polity. *Journal of Cultural Science* 6(1): 71–105.

Hartley, J. and McWilliam, K. (2009) *Story Circle: Digital Storytelling around the World.* Oxford: Wiley.

Lambert, J. (2010) *Digital Storytelling Cookbook.* Berkeley, CA: Digital Diner Press.

Lewis, K. and Matthews, N. (2017) The Afterlife of Capture Wales: Digital Stories and Their Listening Publics. In: Dunford M. and Jenkins T. (eds.) *Digital Storytelling: Form and Content.* London: Palgrave Macmillan UK, pp.103–118.

Lewis, J., Williams, A. and Franklin, B. (2008) A Compromised Fourth Estate? *Journalism Studies* 9(1): 1–20.

Lunch, N. and Lunch, C. (2006) *Insights into Participatory Video*. Oxford: Insight Share.

Lundby, K. (2008) *Digital Storytelling, Mediatized Stories*. New York, NY: Peter Lang.

Martin, C. (2013) *Digital Storytelling Workshop Records Passions for Justice*. Available at: www.denverpost.com/2013/10/05/digital-storytelling-workshop-records-passions-for-justice/ (accessed 22 April 2021).

Matthews, R. (2017) The Socio-Local Newspaper: Creating a Sustainable Future for the Legacy Provincial News Industry. In: Berglez P., Olausson U. and Orts M. (eds.) *Sustainable Journalism*. New York, NY: Peter Lang, pp.333–350.

Mayhew, F. (2019) *UK Local Newspaper Closures: Net Loss of 245 Titles since 2005, New Press Gazette Research*. Available at: www.pressgazette.co.uk/more-than-40-local-news-titles-closed-in-2018-with-loss-of-some-editorial-275-jobs-new-figures-show/ (accessed 27 April 2021).

Mitchell, C., De Lange, N. and Moletsane, R. (2017) *Participatory Visual Methodologies*. London: Sage.

Orchard, R. (2014) The Slow Journalism Revolution. *TEDx Madrid, October 2014*. Available at: www.youtube.com/watch?v=UGtFXtnWME4 (accessed 23 April 2021).

PhotoVoice, (2021) *Care Leavers in Focus (CLiF)*. Available at: https://photovoice.org/care-leavers-in-focus-clif/ (accessed 26 April 2021).

Porter, A. (2007) IMAGEination in Power – The Creative Citizen. In: Dowmunt T., Dunford M. and van Hemert N. (eds.) *Inclusion through Media*. London: Goldsmiths, pp.73–94.

Rauch, J. (2018) *Slow Media: Why Slow Is Satisfying, Sustainable, and Smart*. Oxford: Oxford University Press.

Shapiro, N. (2019) *Daughter of Farmworkers in Quincy, Now a Ph.D. Student Studying Conditions in the Fields, Wins $100,000 Bullitt Prize*. Available at: www.seattletimes.com/seattle-news/child-of-farm-workers-now-a-ph-d-student-studying-conditions-in-the-fields-wins-100000-bullitt-prize/ (accessed 22 April 2021).

Thumim, N. (2012) *Self-Representation and Digital Culture*. London: Palgrave Macmillan.

Index

www.ingramcontent.com/pod-product-compliance
Ingram Content Group UK Ltd.
Pitfield, Milton Keynes, MK11 3LW, UK
UKHW020420010325
455677UK00029B/947

9 781032 001890